RICH BROTT

SO-ACZ-221

A BIBLICAL PERSPECTIVE ON

TITHING
&
GIVING

A Believer's Stewardship Guide

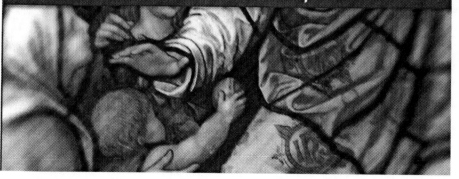

Published by

ABC Book Publishing

AbcBookPublishing.com
Printed in U.S.A.

A Biblical Perspective On Tithing and Giving
A Believer's Stewardship Guide

© Copyright 2008 by Richard A. Brott
10 Digit ISBN: 1-60185-000-X
13 Digit ISBN (EAN): 978-1-60185-000-3

All scripture quotations, unless otherwise indicated, are taken from the *Holy Bible, New International Version®. NIV®.* Copyright © 1973, 1978, 1984 by International Bible Society. Used by permission of Zondervan Publishing House. All rights reserved.

Other Versions used are:

AMP—*Amplified Bible.*

Amer. Std.—American Standard Version, 1901.

KJV—*King James Version. Authorized King James Version.*

NASB—Scripture taken from the *New American Standard Bible,* ©1960, 1962, 1963, 1968, 1971, 1972, 1973, 1975, 1977 by The Lockman Foundation. Used by permission.

NKJV—Scripture taken from the *New King James Version.* Copyright © 1979, 1980, 1982 by Thomas Nelson, Inc. Publishers. Used by permission. All rights reserved.

TLB—Verses marked (TLB) are taken from *The Living Bible* © 1971. Used by permission of Tyndale House Publishers, Inc., Wheaton, IL 60189. All rights reserved.

Scripture taken from *THE MESSAGE: The Bible in Contemporary Language* © 2002 by Eugene H. Peterson. All rights reserved.

This publication is designed to provide interesting reading material and general information with regard to the subject matter covered. It is printed, distributed and sold with the understanding that neither the publisher nor the author is engaged in rendering religious, family, legal, accounting, investing, financial or other professional advice. If any such advice is required, the services of a competent professional person should be sought.

Every effort has been made to supply complete and accurate information. However, neither the publisher nor the author assumes any responsibility for its use, nor for any infringements of patents or other rights of third parties that would result.

First Edition, January 2008
Richard A. Brott
All Rights Reserved

About the Author

Rich Brott holds a Bachelor of Science degree in Business and Economics and a Master of Business Administration.

Rich has served in an executive position with some very successful businesses. He has functioned on the board of directors for churches, businesses, and charities and served on a college advisory board.

He has authored over twenty books:

- *5 Simple Keys to Financial Freedom*
- *10 Life-Changing Attitudes That Will Make You a Financial Success*
- *15 Biblical Responsibilities Leading to Financial Wisdom*
- *30 Biblical Principles for Managing Your Money*
- *35 Keys to Financial Independence*
- *A Biblical Perspective On Tithing & Giving*
- *Basic Principles for Maximizing Your Personal Cash Flow*
- *Basic Principles of Conservative Investing*
- *Biblical Principles for Becoming Debt Free*
- *Biblical Principles for Building a Successful Business*
- *Biblical Principles for Financial Success – Student Workbook*
- *Biblical Principles for Financial Success – Teacher Workbook*
- *Biblical Principles for Personal Evangelism (out of print)*
- *Biblical Principles for Releasing Financial Provision*
- *Biblical Principles for Staying Out of Debt*
- *Biblical Principles for Success in Personal Finance*
- *Biblical Principles That Create Success Through Productivity*
- *Business, Occupations, Professions & Vocations in the Bible*
- *Family Finance Handbook*
- *Family Finance Student Workbook*
- *Family Finance Teacher Workbook*
- *Public Relations for the Local Church (out of print)*

Rich Brott and his wife, Karen, have been married for 35 years. He resides in Portland, Oregon, with his wife, three children, son-in-law and granddaughter.

Dedication

This book is dedicated to the many believers who seek honest answers to sincere questions. In its pages you will understand the basic principle of the tithe, the purpose for its establishment and your stewardship responsibilities toward it. Additionally you will understand your opportunity to enter into God's highest blessing and prosperity through committed giving of yourself, your energy, your time, your talent, abilities and your finances.

Table of Contents

SEGMENT ONE
The Blessing of Tithing

SEGMENT TWO
The Blessing of Giving

Preface

I have met a number of people who adamantly propose that their tithe belongs to whomever they decide to give it. For example, I know of one Christian who faithfully defends this position in that she believes that she is tithing when she gives money to her married children.

Help whomever you wish, but don't confuse the tithe with your other charitable giving. The tithe belongs to your local church. This is where you are fed, sustained and where you have relationships. Only your local church will help you should you one day find yourself in need. Only your local church will see to it that you are visited in the hospital or fed when you are without. God's funding plan for the operation of the local church is His tithe which comes from your increase.

Many people live life just for themselves. Many seek self-fulfillment oblivious to the plight of the world around them. Some seek to become wealthy, not to bless others, but to serve themselves up with the good life. We do well to remember the fact that money and possessions are only temporary. At best, money only lasts a lifetime. At worst, it doesn't last at all. It is very fleeting, only a vapor, just like our lives. Why spend all of your life trying to accumulate something that will never last? How much better it would be for you to spend your time investing in things that are eternal in nature.

Being the recipient of God's provision and blessing and enjoying great wealth and prosperity is not meant for the purpose of accumulating earthly temporary gain. It is to be used to build a foundation for heavenly gain. Instead of hoarding it all for personal enjoyment, it is to be used to further the kingdom of God.

What kind of a giver are you? Are you a person who gives grudgingly or are you the kind of person that God loves; a cheerful giver. A cheerful giver receives great happiness; so much that the giver's own challenges and personal pain is soon forgotten. It is a wonderful life becoming a great giver!

Blessings!

Rich Brott

Introduction

S ometimes we don't realize how blessed we are. We think in terms of new cars, clothes, furniture, the size of our house, the size of our bank account, etc. But Scripture talks about opening up the windows of heaven and pouring out a great blessing. When thinking about this blessing don't make the mistake of forgetting all of the wonderful ways in which you have become the recipient of His love and blessing. True riches is very different than you might think. Having good health and the ability to enjoy one's family, friends and life in general is what real wealth and real blessing is all about. God wants us to be happy and enjoy His creation.

Are we the owners of our money and possessions, or is God? The correct answer is that God owns it all. As Creator of the world and owner of all that it possesses, He is in complete control of everything. God owns the world. God owns me. God owns my money. God owns my possessions. He owns me because He created me. He owns me because He bought me again when He purchased me with His life. I need to acknowledge His ownership!

It is also true that if God owns it all, He has the right to control it all. If He has the right to control all, does He not also have the right to delegate some responsibility to us? The Bible calls us stewards. Our role today is that of manager. A steward or manager is someone that has been put in charge of possessions he or she does not own.

If everything truly comes from God (and it does), then He owns it all. If He owns it all, then we have been placed in charge of possessions that belong to someone else. We, as stewards or managers, are accountable to the owner (God) for the quality of our managing. What kind of results are we producing? How good of a money/possessions manager are you? Is there room for improvement?

What is the level of your faithfulness? Are you asking God for great provision, yet while being unfaithful in the smaller blessings He has allowed to come your way? Joseph, after being sold by his brothers into slavery, suffered a great injustice and could have easily turned his back on God and become a very bitter person. But Joseph provides us with a good example. In spite of all the bad things wished upon him by his half-brothers, he still remained strong because he believed in God.

God honored Joseph for his faithfulness and helped him to be successful in everything he was assigned to do. Because of his faithfulness in carrying out his duties, Pharaoh eventually noticed him and gave him great power. After a series of several events Joseph had the opportunity to forgive his brothers and provide financial aid and blessing to his entire family. God fully vindicated Joseph's faith. After all the years of adversity, God's purpose was accomplished.

Genesis 50:20 sums up the attitude that Joseph had in his statement, "You intended to harm me, but God intended it for good to accomplish what is now being done, the saving of many lives."

Men and women of biblical times, historical times and living today have been and continue to be blessed by God for a particular purpose. God has a purpose for our life; He will bring it to pass. Joseph was a man of humility, God-given talent and wisdom, and a person of purpose. As he submitted his life to the authority of the Almighty, the blessing of God was disbursed through his life and his hands.

When it comes to giving, we must do so in complete confidence that our God will not only meet our needs, but allow us to have plenty left over so that we can joyfully share it with others. When it comes to personal possessions, money and wealth, you cannot take it with you but you CAN send it on ahead. Bottom line is this: what you keep, you will lose, but what you give away, you will gain.

When you become a faithful tither and a generous giver you become an individual whom God can bless. Here is a brief description of such a person.

- Their entire life and community spirit is based on biblical principles.
- They accept 100% of the responsibility for results.
- They are courageous and risk takers.
- They are spiritually aligned.
- They are functionally focused; they know where they are going and how to get it done.
- They are highly decisive; they move things forward continuously.
- They are faithful tithers
- They are impeccably honest.
- They are persistent and committed.
- They have above average ambition.
- They have above-average will power.
- They have tremendous desire; they look at the reward not the challenge.
- They have purpose; and seek to fulfill it.
- They are generous givers.

Nothing happens in the economy of God until you give something away. It is a universal law of God. Paul very appropriately reminds us: "Remember this: Whoever sows sparingly will also reap sparingly, and whoever sows generously will also reap generously" (II Corinthians 9:6 NIV).

Giving is the trigger for God's financial miracles. When you give to the Kingdom of God, it will be given back to you. But where will it come from? Who will give to you? Will God cause money to float down from heaven so that your needs will be met? No. The Bible says, "shall men give into your ....(life)." This is how the cycle of blessing works. When you give to God, He in turn causes others to give to you. Perhaps it will be in the form of new customers to your business, new products to sell, and so on. When God owns your business, He will make sure it prospers.

Bottom line: It's not my word, your pastor's word or the financial needs of your local church. It's God's Word for you today. Get in the flow of God's blessing by following the basic principles of His Word. Your needs will be met, your life will be full and your blessings will be abundant. The happy and prosperous life that you've always dreamed of will become yours.

To faithfulness in giving and your greatest
prosperity and blessing in God!

Rich Brott

SEGMENT ONE

The Blessing of Tithing

CHAPTER 1

It's Not Just About Money

The topic of **Tithing** on your increase and **Giving** generously always relate to your entire life and all that you are concerned with. It's not strictly a financial issue. We have much to give that is far more valuable than money. We have our time, our commitment, our attitude, our gifting, our energy, our service, our talent, our assets, our devotion and our entire life. Yet in all that we have to offer, our attitude toward our finances does play an important role and affects the other areas of our life.

When it comes to the non-monetary resources we have, such as our personal time, biblical stewardship is not about twisting arms and attempting to persuade people to volunteer for needed services. Rather it is about helping people recognize their God-given talents and abilities and helping them move into the giftings they have been blessed with. Once talents have been discovered and giftings acknowledged, it becomes the job of the church to figure out how those personal gifts can be utilized. It's not about volunteerism, but it is about gift mobilization.

Biblical stewardship is not about giving a lot of money just so the church can function in its community role. Yes, the church does need financing for its operational needs and vision mandate. But your role in receiving the blessings of God is all about you keeping only a needed portion of God's blessing and returning a large portion of the blessing so that others can be blessed as well. We should become resourceful and efficient stewards of all the possessions God has sent our way.

Our culture and society have sold us a bill of goods. They teach us that in order to be happy, we have to have certain things. But we must resist the world's view of wealth, happiness, and possessions. We don't have to have it all! We don't have to wear just the right clothes, drive that certain brand of car, have the latest model available, buy a bigger home, possess the latest digital camera, and carry a dozen credit cards in our wallet.

We must not allow our culture to dictate to us its worldview of what our lives should consist of. Our society should not be allowed to design our lifestyle, nor should it tell us what success is and what the picture of affluence should look like. Success is doing what God wants done.

Wealth is having only what you need to exist. A rich man or woman is one who has one penny more than he or she needs. Wealth is more than money. It is having a local church that inspires you to draw close to God. It is having a loving spouse and the blessing of children. Wealth is enjoying great health and great relationships. Wealth is having good friends. Wealth is receiving salvation and God's gift of eternal life with Him. ⚭

CHAPTER 2

Tithing is Returning the Tenth

It is such a blessing to be a generous giver! Your tithe is the first part of your giving commitment. When you give with joy and give with all your heart, you are not concerned so much with giving an amount of minimal acceptance. But tithing of our increase is a very real minimum giving opportunity necessary even for this generation.

Genesis 28:20–22

Then Jacob made a vow, saying, "If God will be with me and will watch over me on this journey I am taking and will give me food to eat and clothes to wear so that I return safely to my father's house, then the LORD will be my God and this stone that I have set up as a pillar will be God's house, and of all that you give me I will give you a tenth."

Early in biblical history we see a picture of Jacob, a man who promised God that he would return a tenth of all his increase. Jacob was beginning a journey, apparently leaving his family for a period of time, making his bed under the stars. God came to him in a dream, promising him great blessings in the future, which of course He gave. Jacob promised the tenth, as he understood the principle of the tenth.

THERE ARE MANY REASONS FOR TITHING.

1. God is training us to be faithful stewards in handling money.

People who do not pay a tithe, or tenth, of their income often have poor financial habits that leave them broke soon after payday. Tithing teaches us to pay that which we owe first. Our financial obligation to God is first priority. When He blesses us with increase, He expects us to give a minimum of 10 percent as a tithe into the "storehouse," which in definition is our local church. We should be cheerful givers! We should give out of our abundance. We should give out of our love. And we should give to meet the needs of those who do not have and find themselves in lack.

2. God is teaching us the principle concerning the cycle of money.

We reap what we sow, and God is training us to plant some "seed money" in tithing so that He will have cause to abundantly bless us. In the same way that just one seed can multiply itself many times over, so it is with money. Certainly our investments should include investing in God's work.

3. The tithe belongs to God (Leviticus 27:30).

It is already His, and if we withhold it we are robbing Him (Malachi 3:8). Robbery is taking that which belongs to another for personal use, either by fraud or violence. It is not only taking what is not yours, but also keeping back for yourself what belongs to someone else. One-tenth of your income belongs to God, and failure to pay that debt is robbery. When we rob God, we permit something to have stronger power over us than His will does. When we retain God's money in our treasuries, we will find it a losing proposition. How can a person not pay tithes? Can we afford to be so selfish as not to give God His small part, especially when it was all His to begin with? Can we hold a tight fist in the face of God, who has freely given us all things (Romans 8:32)?

4. Tithing is commanded.

Malachi 3:10 says, "Bring ye all the tithes into the storehouse." Tithing, as established by Abraham, involves giving 10 percent of one's earnings.

5. Abraham tithed before the law of Moses.

The first biblical record of tithing is found in Genesis 14. Abram's nephew, Lot, was taken captive in a battle between some kings and their armies. When Abram set out to rescue him, not only was he successful, but he also brought back a large amount of spoils. Genesis 14:11–20 records this event.

This Old Testament account of the first mention of tithing indicates that the spoils belonged to Abram by right of conquest. Abram has been called the "father of the faithful" (Romans 4), and his life is exemplary to us today, his faith a prototype for all believers. In this passage we are told that Melchizedek was the "priest of God Most High." Verse 19 notes that Abram was also "of the most high God" (KJV). And we are told that the most high God is "possessor of heaven and earth" (v. 19, KJV). Apparently, tithing in this context was a direct acknowledgment of the sovereignty and lordship of God over all the earth. Giving God back a tenth of what is already His anyway was a way of acknowledging God's ownership of the entire earth's wealth. Haggai 2:8 declares, "The silver is mine, and the gold is mine, saith the LORD of hosts" (KJV).

If God cannot trust you with the first portion, how can He give you future destiny?

6. The New Testament recounts the first tithe.

Hebrews 7:1–19 records the same story as Genesis 14. This is the last direct reference to tithing in the New Testament, and it seems interesting to me that it also refers to the first reference found in the Old Testament. Abraham gave tithes to Melchizedek long before the Mosaic law was given by God at Mount Sinai. Abraham honored the Most High God by freely giving from a loving, grateful heart. It was a true act of worship. Abraham's giving was not based on the law but on a grateful response to God's grace. You can give without loving, but you cannot love without giving!

7. A "tithe" is a tenth.

The "tithe" simply means the "tenth." A tenth is 10 percent. A ratio of one to ten is easy to remember and easy to figure—much like our decimal system today. It seems natural and logical to divide things into tens.

- Tithing is scriptural.

- Tithing is systematic.

- Tithing is simple.

- Tithing is successful.

- Tithing is right.

God has ordained that the use of money is related to spiritual values. The only way to get our treasures into heaven is to put them into something that is going to heaven. Cattle, lands, stocks, bonds, and houses will not make it to heaven. Only men, women, boys, and girls of all color are going to heaven. By exchanging our earthly possessions and money into the saving of souls, we will take our acquired wealth with us to an eternal home.

8. The tithe is the first part.

The tithe is the first part of our income. It is to be set apart before the rent, before the bills, and before we go shopping because it belongs to God and He must come first in our lives. We are to give it to the Lord as a token of gratefulness, recognizing that He is the originator of all our income.

Deuteronomy 26:10

And now, behold, I have brought the firstfruits of the land which you, O LORD, have given me." Then you shall set it before the LORD your God, and worship before the LORD your God.

9. Tithing does away with hit-and-miss methods of giving.

If a person is truly tithing, it is a systematic giving of 10 percent of all earnings to the Lord's work. If we earn ten dollars, one dollar of it is given back to God, and we are allowed to live on the remaining 90 percent. Some may think that if they gave God an occasional tenth, this would be enough. But people cannot be counted as tithers unless they consistently give a tenth.

The Bible teaches that tithing is to be the minimum of one's giving, not the maximum.

Just because one gives a tenth does not necessarily mean he has fulfilled his stewardship responsibility to God. We are to put God first and show that He is most important to us by tithing the firstfruits of our income. First means that which is before anything else in the order of time, before all others in place and in consideration. Traditionally, the "firstfruits" is the fruit or produce first matured and collected in season. All we are, all we possess, and all we earn are equally the gifts of God. We are to acknowledge God as giver of all good things, which are the support and comfort of our natural lives, and therefore we are to give to God our first and our best.

I don't know how the Lord does it, but I have seen it work in my life over and over. I've seen the Lord bless the nine-tenths after the tithe until it went further than the full amount would have if I had withheld the first tenth.

Wthen we give God our firstfruits, He multiplies it back to us many times over.

10. Jesus Christ endorsed tithing.

Jesus Christ did not repeal the law concerning tithing; instead, He endorsed it. Tithe paying was a general practice during the time of Christ. In the New Testament, the term *tithe(s)* is found ten times. The sect that was strictest concerning tithing was the Pharisees. In order to be admitted into the fellowship of the Pharisees, one was obligated to pay his tithe. He was obligated to tithe to the treasury what he bought, what he sold, and what he ate. Three of the references are found in the Gospels. Jesus faced the question of tithing. If He had not been a tither, this would have been one of the first complaints of the Pharisees. They continually watched His every word and action, seeking to find fault with Him, but they never once pointed to a lack of tithing.

The fact that Jesus Christ was admitted into the homes of the Pharisees for meals is evidence that He was a tither. Luke 11:37 says, "As he spake, a certain Pharisee besought him to dine with him: and he went in, and sat down to meat" (KJV). It was definitely against the vow of a Pharisee to be the host of an outsider. In Luke 18:22, Christ did not offer disapproval to the Pharisee who said, "I give tithes of all that I possess," nor was He finding fault in his tithe paying. Jesus was condemning this attitude of self-righteousness and egotism.

11. Becoming a tither.

If you have not been tithing, according to Scripture you have been robbing God. Thankfully, we can walk in the promises of God. One such promise is that God *will* forgive us when we confess our sins. God is ready to forgive you today of any unrighteousness on your part with regards to the tithe. He is ready to pour out blessing on your life as He opens His storehouse to us.

1 John 1:9

If we confess our sins, He is faithful and just to forgive us our sins and to cleanse us from all unrighteousness.

God has issued an invitation to prove the Lord's promises, to test Him with our tithe. He virtually offers a guaranteed direct and abundant return on your investment into His kingdom. This return comes in the form of His blessing. When we tithe, we can contend for God's promises.

12. Promises to the tither.

There are many promises in God's Word for those who tithe faithfully. The command to tithe in Malachi 3:10 is followed up by some great promises. As we tithe, the Lord's response is to open for us the windows of heaven. Verse 11 says that He pours out for us "such blessing that there will not be room enough to receive it"! Tithing activates this great blessing in our lives.

This verse goes on to promise that God will rebuke the devourer for our sakes so that the fruit of our ground will not be destroyed and the vine *will* bear fruit for us in the field. When we tithe, God personally goes to bat for us against the enemy of our soul with regards to our finances. We can be sure that when we sow, we will bear fruit. He causes our ground and fields to prosper. Who wouldn't like to see the hand of God at work in our workplace as we watch in wonder at how God causes the fruit of our labor to prosper?

When the blessing of God falls on us in such a mighty way, we can be sure that it won't go unnoticed. Malachi 3:12 shares the result of this great blessing: "'And all nations will call you blessed, For you will be a delightful land,' Says the LORD of hosts." How exciting that this blessing will not only be noticeable to us, but also to our coworkers, neighbors, and families.

Proverbs 28:20

A faithful man will abound with blessings, but he who hastens to be rich will not go unpunished.

As we are faithful and test God in this area, let's trust Him to fulfill His promises. Be abundantly blessed! ❧

CHAPTER 3

Your Tithing Questions...Answered

WHAT IS TITHING?

A tithe is a debt owed. It refers to the tenth of our increase that already belongs to God. It is not ours to keep. We pay it as we would any other debt. Debts are paid, not given. There are consequences to unpaid debt. In the context of tithing, the inaction of unpaid debt results in the action of "robbery." In Scripture, the only way man can rob God is by not returning the tenth that is already His to begin with.

Malachi 3:8

Will a man rob God? Yet you rob me. "But you ask, 'How do we rob you?' In tithes and offerings."

One of the biggest tests in the walk of many people is the command to tithe. It is a spiritual test. God owns everything according to the Bible. And anything that we have by way of possessions is simply because God allows us to have them.

Exodus 19:5

Now therefore, if ye will obey my voice indeed, and keep my covenant, then ye shall be a peculiar treasure unto me above all people: for all the earth is mine. (KJV)

Psalm 50:12

If I were hungry I would not tell you, for the world is mine, and all that is in it. Although the Lord already owns everything, He does allow us to keep a significant part of the fruit of our labor. He gives us the greater portion — the 90 percent. And with our obedience, God promises to bless us when we tithe! When you tithe, He will make the 90 percent stretch further than the whole 100 percent should you keep it in disobedience.

WHAT IS THE PREMISE FOR TITHING?

The Old Testament believers were required to give a specific amount of money in order to meet the needs of the ministry, the poor, etc. While the New Testament does not specifically mention the tithe as a directive, 2 Corinthians 8:3 does direct us to give as we are able and even above and beyond. Jesus' view on giving was even more radical than tithing! He did not want us to be bound by material things and even said that we should sell our possessions and give all to the poor.

Luke told us to accumulate our treasures in heaven, where they would be safe from moths and thieves. When you look closely, the tithe of 10 percent seems like a minimum giving guideline in the New Testament. The new did not replace the old, but it increased and expanded the giving possibilities.

WHEN WAS THE FIRST TITHE GIVEN?

Abraham tithed before the law of Moses. The first biblical record of tithing is found in Genesis 14. Abram's nephew, Lot, was taken captive in a battle between some kings and their armies. When

Abram set out to rescue him, not only was he successful, but he also brought back a large amount of spoils. Genesis 14:11–20 records this event.

Giving God back a tenth of what was already His was a way of acknowledging God's ownership of the entire earth's wealth. Haggai 2:8 declares, "The silver is mine, and the gold is mine, saith the LORD of hosts" (KJV). Long before the time of Moses, the dedication of the tenth to God was recognized as a duty. It was consecrated and set apart for special purposes.

WAS TITHING COMMANDED IN THE PATRIARCHAL DAYS?

Yes, please note the following Scriptures on this topic:

Genesis 14:20

"And blessed be God Most High, who delivered your enemies into your hand." Then Abram gave him a tenth of everything.

Genesis 28:22

And this stone that I have set up as a pillar will be God's house, and of all that you give me I will give you a tenth.

Leviticus 27:30

A tithe of everything from the land, whether grain from the soil or fruit from the trees, belongs to the LORD; it is holy to the LORD.

Leviticus 27:32

The entire tithe of the herd and flock—every tenth animal that passes under the shepherd's rod—will be holy to the LORD.

When you say to "tithe," how much is that?

The *tithe* simply means the "tenth." A tenth is 10 percent. A ratio of one to ten is easy to remember and easy to figure—much like our decimal system today. It seems natural and logical to divide things into tens. God intended that the use of money be related to spiritual values.

How should I calculate and pay my tithes?

Your first calculation is to figure your increase. That might be from a paycheck, bonuses, or the sale of some property. When you think "increase," it becomes easier to figure God's tithe. After figuring out how much increase you have received, calculate the tithe, or the tenth. God's portion of your increase is 10 percent. You keep the 90 percent, you pay the 10 percent.

Is the tithe always money?

No! Money is certainly a necessary part of it (i.e. our employment paychecks, bonuses, etc.). However, our "increase" is often more than money. It could be non-monetary increases such as real estate, stocks, or simply vegetables grown in our garden.

When should I tithe?

You should tithe just as soon as you receive the increase. In the New Testament, the apostle Paul laid out a plan to the saints in Galatia and also to the Corinthian church. This was meant to bring some order and consistency to their giving. Simply put, he told them to hold out their tithe whenever they were paid and to present it on the first day of the week set aside for their worship. This was not only meant for continuity and regularity, but also for simplicity and convenience for them as they gathered for worship on the first day of the week.

1 Corinthians 16:1–2

Now about the collection for God's people: Do what I told the Galatian churches to do. On the first day of every week, each one of you should set aside a sum of money in keeping with his income, saving it up, so that when I come no collections will have to be made.

WHERE SHOULD I GIVE MY TITHE?

The Bible teaches us to bring our tithes to the "storehouse." The Old Testament storehouse was the place God designated to keep His abundance and to distribute it to the people. It was also His tabernacle where His name was established. Today, a storehouse is your local church, the place where you receive your spiritual food, nurturing, and fellowship—the place you call home.

God does not need your money in heaven. In heaven there are no unsaved that need to be evangelized. There are no poor who need food. There are no needy who need shelter. No sick people who need health care. No need for counseling facilities or housing for the homeless.

Your tithe should be given to your local church. This is where you are fed, watered, and cared for. If you or a family member becomes ill, it is the local church who will visit you in the hospital, bring meals to your bedside, send flowers and cards of encouragement. Only the local church can help the elderly with yard work and other special needs. Only the local church can help out with food baskets for the single parent, senior citizen, or the family that has suffered a job loss. It is the local church and its ministries that extend both practical and spiritual food.

WHO NEEDS TO TITHE?

Everyone who is of an age that they understand the purpose, principle, and meaning of the tenth should tithe. The tenth is a measurement of our sacrifice to God. While God does not need our money,

He does desire our hearts. James says in 1:17 that every good gift comes from above. God wants to bless us spiritually, financially, and in so many other ways. But He needs our hearts first.

Paying our tithes and giving our offerings are very important principles for Christians to follow. We honor God in our faithfulness in these areas. Our money represents a big part of our heart and our life. When we honor God in this principle—the principle of setting aside the first tenth—it says to the world that God is first in our lives. It tells God that we belong to Him first and foremost. When we place Him first, not only will our needs be met according to His promises, but an overflow of blessings from heaven to earth will be released on our behalf.

Do I HAVE TO TITHE? Is TITHING VOLUNTARY? Is IT MANDATORY FOR SALVATION?

While highly recommended, tithing is not a salvation issue. But this is like asking, "Do I *have* to buy my children Christmas presents?" or, "Do I *have* to buy flowers for my wife on our anniversary?" or, "Do I *have* to brush my teeth every day?" or "Do I *have* to take a bath?" Well, no you don't *have* to do any of these things, but I *do* recommend it. Instead of asking the question, "Do I have to tithe?" the issue should be "Thank God that I *can* tithe, that I *can* have the blessings of God in my daily life!"

WHAT IF I CAN'T AFFORD TO TITHE?

You can't afford *not* to tithe. Your difficulty may not be a "earning" problem, but a "spending" problem. When you spend first and give second, your priorities are out of focus. With the right focus, tithing is never a problem. Malachi 3:10 shows us the only way in the Bible for us to *test* God—we test him with our tithing.

His blessing allows us to decide what to do with 90 percent of our increase; why would you want to be cursed over 10 percent that does not belong to you anyway? I want to live on the 90 percent that is blessed by God. Hebrews 11:16 notes that we cannot please

God without faith. When you are walking with Him, it's all about obedience, faith, and trust. You walk in faith, not by your own personal insights.

Faith says to God that your trust in Him is so great that you believe your 90 percent will stretch further with God than 100 percent that you alone are directing. If you think that waiting until you can afford to tithe is right, then you will never feel like you can afford it. If we are all to get through life in good stead, we for sure need the supernatural provision and blessing of God. God is faithful...so give Him a try!

WHAT DOES MONEY HAVE TO DO WITH BEING A CHRISTIAN?

Money is a very sensitive issue in our culture even though we are among the most blessed in the world. Often we become very attached to money because of the luxuries in life it brings to us. Yet money is very central to our spiritual experience. Our willingness (or unwillingness) to part with it represents our commitment to Jesus Christ. It is often a measuring stick of our Christian walk. Sometimes we become impatient with our wealth.

When I refer to *wealth*, I'm referring to having much more than enough. When I say *impatient*, I mean it in the sense that we always want more. The more we have, the more we want. As we give in to selfishness and lack of discipline when it comes to matters of money, we become bad stewards of all that God has entrusted to our care. Regardless of how we spend our money, it will not be with us forever.

1 Timothy 6:7–10

For we brought nothing into the world, and we can take nothing out of it. But if we have food and clothing, we will be content with that. People who want to get rich fall into temptation and a trap and into many foolish and harmful desires that plunge men into ruin and destruction. For the love of money is a root

of all kinds of evil. Some people, eager for money, have wan-
dered from the faith and pierced themselves with many griefs.

This verse not only reminds us of our temporary use of worldly possessions, but also that we should be content with food and shelter. Many of the world's population do not have enough of either. The verse also tells of the destructive effects upon a person's life resulting from the love of money. It's pretty plain talk. Some people who love money leave the faith and heap grief upon their life.

Hebrews 13:5

Keep your lives free from the love of money and be content with what you have, because God has said, "Never will I leave you; never will I forsake you."

We are advised and counseled that we should continually examine ourselves to be certain that we are not in love with money. Our motives and decisions must be pure. Money is a means, not an end all. This verse infers that we are not to be focused on gain, but we are to be content because we are in the care of Almighty God. To be discontent is to distrust God's care. To be discontent is to distrust God's power.

CAN A PERSON STEAL FROM GOD?

Malachi 3:8 asks the question, "Will a man rob God?" Kind of a thought-provoking question isn't it! In today's language, the question would be: "Are you a thief?" If you are a tither, you may still be just 1 percent short of being a thief. Malachi goes on to say in verse 10, "Bring ye all the tithes into the storehouse." In 1 Corinthians, 16:2, Paul says, "Let every one of you lay by him in store, as God hath prospered him." This was an obvious reference to the tithe.

Tithing and renewal go hand in hand because tithes provide for the release of ministry in the house of God as seen throughout the Old Testament. Nehemiah, seeing the lack of support for the Levites and the house of God forsaken, contended for the tithe in Nehemiah 13:10–12. Ministry was being prevented because the servants of God had no provision when the people stopped tithing. They were forced to return to their own fields, leaving the house of God without ministers. As affirmed by 1 Corinthians 9:1–11, those being ministered to are to provide for those who are ministering.

God considers giving so important that John 3:16 records, "For God so loved the world, that he gave his only begotten Son, that whosoever believeth in him should not perish, but have everlasting life" (KJV).

MY TITHING WON'T AMOUNT TO MUCH. WHY DOES GOD NEED MY TITHE?

Of course, we know that God does not need any money at all. But He does need our obedience. The widow of Mark 12:41 gave all she had. Whatever we give, either the tenth or beyond the tenth, should be given from the start, off the top, before we commit to anything else. Proverbs 3:9 directs us to honor the Lord from our wealth by giving the first of all our produce: "Honor the LORD with your wealth, with the firstfruits of all your crops."

WHAT IF I CHOOSE NOT TO TITHE?

God has a name for non-tithers. He calls them robbers. He says that they are cursed.

Malachi 3:8–9

Will a man rob God? Yet you have robbed Me! But you say, "In what way have we robbed You?" In tithes and offerings. You are cursed with a curse, For you have robbed Me.

WHAT DO I GET IN RETURN FOR TITHING?

Your needs will always be met. God will see to it that you always have shelter, never go hungry and that you will be on the receiving end of the hand of God.

2 Corinthians 9:6–11

*Remember this: Whoever sows sparingly will also reap spar-
ingly, and whoever sows generously will also reap generously....
And God is able to make all grace abound to you, so that in all
things at all times, having all that you need, you will abound
in every good work. As it is written: "He has scattered abroad
his gifts to the poor; his righteousness endures forever." Now
he who supplies seed to the sower and bread for food will also
supply and increase your store of seed and will enlarge the harvest of your righteousness. You will be made rich in every way
so that you can be generous on every occasion, and through us
your generosity will result in thanksgiving to God.*

SHOULD I TITHE ON AN INHERITANCE?

Yes. An inheritance is an increase. Therefore you must tithe on everything that comes into your possession in that way. When Abraham returned with the spoils of war after the successful defeat of
Chedorlaomer and the kings (Genesis 14:17–20), he immediately
paid the tithe.

I AM SELF-EMPLOYED. HOW SHOULD I TITHE?

If you work for an hourly wage, you should return a tenth of that
to the Lord. If you earn twenty dollars per hour, you must tithe two
dollars for every compensated hour. If you are a contractor who
builds decks, sheds, buildings, etc., you would tithe on your increase. Your increase would be your gross sale, less your expenses
(materials, permits, etc.).

If you are a farmer, you would tithe on proceeds from the sale
of the grain, less the cost of the seed, etc. If you are an investor, you
would tithe on the sales of your investment (land, house, property,
stocks, bonds, etc.), less your initial investment expense.

Deuteronomy 14:22

Thou shalt truly tithe all the increase of thy seed, that the field bringeth forth year by year. (KJV)

DO I TITHE ON MY TAX REFUND?

That depends. If you have been tithing throughout the year on your net, then you certainly must tithe on the monies received from your state and federal return of excess dollars paid. If you have been tithing on your gross income each week (recommended), then it is not necessary to tithe a second time on the same increase. However, monies received via government tax refunds provide an excellent opportunity to give love offerings or special designated offerings to worthy local church projects.

I HAVE A LOT OF DEBT.

No doubt, we can give ourselves a variety of excuses why we just cannot tithe and give offerings. It is very easy to rationalize our reasons for disobedience. It is a very simple decision. Are you going to obey His command or disobey?

SHOULD I BEGIN TITHING IF I CANNOT MEET MY PRESENT OBLIGATIONS USING 100 PERCENT OF MY INCOME?

It is clear that you have a problem. If it is not due to unavoidable health-care debt or any other unforeseen event, then you certainly need to chat with a nonprofit credit counseling service. Free credit counseling services are available. Your pastor can help you locate one. You may be in financial bondage because of uncontrolled, undisciplined spending habits...often the result of a selfish lifestyle.

If you find yourself overwhelmed with debt, there is not an easy way out. You need practical help and spiritual help. What we sow we reap. Your lifestyle of living beyond your means must cease. But you need to begin to work on the spiritual side of things as well. To tithe with heavy debt does require an act of faith. But faith begins with obedience.

God is very clear on the requirement of tithing and is equally clear in His desire to bless your life. He says that when you tithe, He will rebuke the devourer from your life. In other words, He will keep those losses at bay, financial and otherwise, so that the increase in your life will actually increase in purchasing power. He says to "test" Him and see. God truly is waiting in the wings, wishing you would give it a try. He wants to work a miracle in your financial and spiritual life.

DIDN'T JESUS SAY THAT
CERTAIN PEOPLE WILL ALWAYS BE POOR?

Jesus never said that. On the other hand, Christ did say that the poor would always be with us.

Matthew 26:11

"For you always have the poor with you." (NASB)

Jesus was not saying that some people will always be poor. He was not saying that some cultures will always be poor. Nor was He saying that the people of some nations will always be poor; He never said "once poor, always poor."

But He *was* confirming a truth of the world—at any given time there will be poor people. Why is this? Life dictates different seasons for all. All people go through certain times in their life when ill health, lack of employment, unforeseen circumstances, etc., can take away all but the very necessities of life.

There are peaks and valleys in our personal world. Wars come and go. Nations rise and fall. The economies of the nations contract and expand. There are good times and bad times. Life happens. One way to keep struggling without light at the end of your personal financial tunnel is to withhold from God.

2 Corinthians 9:9–11

As it is written: "He has scattered abroad his gifts to the poor; his righteousness endures forever." Now he who supplies seed to the sower and bread for food will also supply and increase your store of seed and will enlarge the harvest of your righteousness. You will be made rich in every way so that you can be generous on every occasion, and through us your generosity will result in thanksgiving to God.

WHAT IS THE DIFFERENCE BETWEEN THE "TITHE" AND GIVING AN "OFFERING"?

The tithe is 10 percent of your increase. According to Deuteronomy, this already belongs to God. It is not yours to spend; it is His alone. An offering is any gift presented to God *above* the tithe. It is ours to give. Whatever the amount, our offerings are reflections of our gratitude for all that we receive from our heavenly Father. This includes our salvation and spiritual blessings; our family, children, health, shelter, and food; and all of our provision and blessings.

2 Corinthians 9:7

Each man should give what he has decided in his heart to give, not reluctantly or under compulsion, for God loves a cheerful giver.

Anything outside of the prescribed percentage that already belongs to God represents an offering of love. An offering is not a predetermined percentage. Our offerings become a measure of our love and appreciation for things of the kingdom.

DOES GOD REALLY WANT TO BLESS ME AS A RESULT OF MY TITHING?

Certainly! However unless you give the tenth due Him, His blessings cannot be unlocked. Obedience triggers the blessing of God. The widow gave all that she had. Whatever we give, either the tenth or beyond the tenth, should be given from the start, off the top, before we commit to anything else.

In Galatians 6:7, Paul tells us that we should not be deceived by thinking anything other than what we sow we will reap. When we sow disobedience, we reap that harvest. When we sow with our obedience, we reap the many blessings of God.

I have heard that tithing was mandated in the Old Testament under the law, but in the New Testament we are under grace. Is it still true for us today?

Let me refer you to a Scripture found in Matthew: "Do not think that I have come to abolish the Law or the Prophets; I have not come to abolish them but to fulfill them." (5:17)

We can infer that Jesus did not do away with the principle of tithing, but expected it to continue into the future. There are those in the Christian world who inaccurately believe that only the Jewish law required one to tithe and that it cannot be for us today.

But according to Galatians 3:17, the law did not come until 430 years after God instituted tithing through Abraham. And, of course, the law did not invalidate previous covenants ratified by God.

Another example is found in Deuteronomy 5. This listing of the Ten Commandments was good then and is certainly applicable to us today. The tithe was given before the law of Moses and is a theme of our faith, not of the law.

It is not a matter of complying with the law, but a matter of building our faith. When properly entered into, this principle of faith releases our personal financial world from the natural economy of this earth and propels it into God's supernatural economy.

What did Jesus teach concerning tithing?

Jesus Christ endorsed tithing. Jesus Christ did not repeal the law concerning tithing. Instead, He endorsed it. Tithe paying was a general practice during the time of Christ. In the New Testament, the term *tithe(s)* is found ten times.

The sect that was strictest concerning tithing was the Pharisees. In order to be admitted into the fellowship of the Pharisees, one was obligated to pay his tithe. He was obligated to tithe to the treasury what he bought, what he sold, and what he ate. Jesus commended the Pharisees for tithing in Matthew 23:23. Tithing was about the only thing they were doing right.

Luke 11:42

"But woe to you Pharisees! For you tithe mint and rue and all manner of herbs, and pass by justice and the love of God. These you ought to have done, without leaving the others undone." (NKJV)

Though tithing is not a requirement for salvation, the love of God and the judgment of sin are. The Lord notes that the Pharisees had selective principles that they chose to obey. Jesus said not to leave the tithing undone; rather tithe, and in addition to tithing, recognize the love of God.

In Luke 16:11, Jesus says that if one has not been faithful in the use of his money, how can he expect God to trust him with great riches. He suggests that the principle of obedience is important no matter the amount of sacrifice.

He also said in Matthew 6:20 that we are to lay up for ourselves treasures in heaven, that when we give our tithe and offerings to the work of the Lord, we are investing in souls for the kingdom. Where else in the New Testament is the "tenth" mentioned?

Luke 18:12

"'I fast twice a week and give a tenth of all I get.'"

Matthew 23:23

"Woe to you, teachers of the law and Pharisees, you hypocrites! You give a tenth of your spices-mint, dill and cummin. But you

have neglected the more important matters of the law-justice, mercy and faithfulness. You should have practiced the latter, without neglecting the former."

Jesus was not saying that one should not tithe; He was saying that in addition to all of the outward issues the Pharisees were addressing, they also needed also to be concerned with issues of the heart. Mercy and faith should be practiced along with tithing.

Hebrews 7:8

Here mortal men receive tithes, but there he receives them, of whom it is witnessed that he lives. (NKJV)

The New Testament references tithing in the present tense, not the past tense.

1 Corinthians 16:2

On the first day of every week, each one of you should set aside a sum of money in keeping with his income, saving it up, so that when I come no collections will have to be made.

This New Testament verse and others like it would seem to strongly indicate that the principle of tithing was a common practice. While the specific word *tithe* is not used here, the presumption is certainly implied. It refers to the first day of the week. It notes that we should lay in store "as God hath prospered" (KJV).

To whom does the tithe belong?

The tithe belongs to God. We "pay," or "return," the tithe. The remaining 90 percent (or 100 percent of what belongs to us) provides us with an opportunity to give offerings. Our "giving" does not start until the tithe has been paid. Our offerings are accepted not by the amount, but by the spirit and attitude in which we give them. The tithe has very little to do with attitude, but has everything to do with obedience.

WHAT SHOULD MY TITHING ATTITUDE BE?

Perhaps you feel that tithing is just a requirement that must be met. But tithing should be done with joy and peace. It should be an expression of your love. To tithe without joy is to view salvation as a requirement for eternal life, but not to expect any of the blessings God has for His children. Jesus Christ freely gave His life for your redemption and certainly wants to bless you in very practical ways. Give Him an opportunity to do so!

In the four Gospels, Jesus talks about money issues more than salvation issues. Doesn't this tell you that He knows how greedy and selfish we can be? Surely He knew that we hold on to that which we cannot ultimately keep. Greed comes from selfishness.

Matthew 16:26

"What good will it be for a man if he gains the whole world, yet forfeits his soul? Or what can a man give in exchange for his soul?"

1 Timothy 6:10

For the love of money is a root of all kinds of evil. Some people, eager for money, have wandered from the faith and pierced themselves with many griefs.

It is not about how much money you have; it's about how much money has you. In the end it all comes down to this: The money you spend is gone. The money you keep will someday be gone as you pass from this world to another. The money you give to the Lord is an investment in the kingdom that you take with you when you go.

It's not about how much money you give. It's about your attitude toward money. Don't let your money or possessions become your master. Don't let them dictate your actions and future.

Matthew 6:24

"No one can serve two masters. Either he will hate the one and love the other, or he will be devoted to the one and despise the other. You cannot serve both God and Money."

A bit of advice here—just be faithful in your tithing and giving of offerings. Every day, day in and day out. Be consistent. Be regular. Be timely. Faithfulness is a great virtue in life.
What does obedience have to do with tithing?

Some people "tip," but don't tithe. They give a little here and a little there. There is no consistency to their faithfulness. They eat the seed that God could be using use to get them out of debt, bless their business, and bring favor upon their family.

Leviticus 27:30–33

A tithe of everything from the land, whether grain from the soil or fruit from the trees, belongs to the LORD; it is holy to the LORD. If a man redeems any of his tithe, he must add a fifth of the value to it. The entire tithe of the herd and flock—every tenth animal that passes under the shepherd's rod—will be holy to the LORD. He must not pick out the good from the bad or make any substitution. If he does make a substitution, both the animal and its substitute become holy and cannot be redeemed.'

People who do not tithe have forgotten to whom it belongs. They refuse to believe that it is all God's money anyway and all He is asking for is the tenth. If you will give God the tenth, He will make sure that the other 90 percent gets you more in the end. God wants us to bring the firstfruits of our labor to Him. He lets us know what can happen to our money if greed plays a role in our life.

Matthew 6:19–21

"Do not store up for yourselves treasures on earth, where moth and rust destroy, and where thieves break in and steal. But

store up for yourselves treasures in heaven, where moth and rust do not destroy, and where thieves do not break in and steal. For where your treasure is, there your heart will be also."

Malachi 3:10–11

"Bring the whole tithe into the storehouse, that there may be food in my house. Test me in this," says the LORD Almighty, "and see if I will not throw open the floodgates of heaven and pour out so much blessing that you will not have room enough for it. I will prevent pests from devouring your crops, and the vines in your fields will not cast their fruit," says the LORD Almighty.

Within the kingdom of God, everything revolves around obedience and choice. You can choose to disobey, ignore the principles of the kingdom, and receive a curse upon your finances—that is to say a plugging up of the conduit of God's blessings upon your finances and life. Alternately you can choose to believe God, be faithful to His Word, act upon His Word through obedience, and be blessed. It is all about attitude and obedience. Do you trust God with your life or not?

God's tithe belongs to your local church. I have met a number of people who adamantly propose that their tithe belongs to whomever they decide to give it. One longtime Christian who faithfully defends the cause of tithing, believes that she is tithing when she gives money to her married children. Of course, there are many people with many needs. Then you have those who somehow drop into your life, whether in person or via the media, who have their hands out.

Help whomever you wish, but don't confuse the tithe with your other charitable giving. The tithe belongs to your local church. This is where you are fed, sustained, and have relationships. Only they will help you should you one day find yourself in need. Only your local church will see to it that you are visited in the hospital or fed when you are without. God's funding plan for the operation of the local church is His tithe, which comes from your increase.

HOW AM I BLESSED BY BEING OBEDIENT?

You are blessed in that God now has the opportunity to unstop the dam that has been holding back His blessing on your life. Obedience triggers the promises of God's Word. Just remember, Satan desires to steal everything good in your life. But God desires to bless you with every good gift from on high. Many Scriptures support both premises.

John 10:10

"The thief comes only to steal and kill and destroy; I have come that they may have life, and have it to the full."

James 1:17

Every good and perfect gift is from above, coming down from the Father of the heavenly lights, who does not change like shifting shadows.

The "devourer," or Satan, who is your spiritual enemy, would love to steal from you. He would love to steal your financial blessing, your family blessing, your wife and children, and your future from you. By being obedient, not only will God bless you, but He promises to hold Satan away from ruining your life. The bottom line is this: Until you have given the tenth (the whole tithe) back to God, which He says belongs to Him alone, your giving cannot begin. If you are obedient in your tithing, God will supply all of your needs.

Philippians 4:19

And my God shall supply all your need according to His riches in glory by Christ Jesus. (NKJV)

After obedience in tithing, you can begin giving offerings because your heart is right. Your offerings will bring God's abundance into your life. Malachi 3:10 describes this abundance as overflowing blessings from heaven.

DIDN'T I EARN MY MONEY FROM WORKING HARD?

Deuteronomy 8:17–18

> *You may say to yourself, "My power and the strength of my hands have produced this wealth for me." But remember the LORD your God, for it is he who gives you the ability to produce wealth, and so confirms his covenant, which he swore to your forefathers, as it is today.*

Every ability you have comes as a gift from God. Your ability to work, to be healthy, and to enjoy life is nothing short of the grace of God. Your accumulation of material goods, your possessions, your wealth, your blessings all come from God. If you can grasp this little bit of understanding, your entire attitude in life will change. You must guard against any false attitude or thoughts that you had anything to do with gaining any wealth. That assumption is completely false. Did you work hard as enabled by your Creator? Of course. Were you a diligent laborer? Certainly. But as the Scripture clearly points out, it is Go alone that gives you the ability (strength, wisdom, knowledge, health, etc.) to produce wealth.

WHERE IS THE ONLY PLACE IN THE BIBLE WHERE WE ARE TOLD TO "TEST" GOD?

There is only one reference in Scripture where we are told to test God to see if the principle really works. It's like God knows we are skeptical in this area so He throws out an honest challenge to us. He says, "Okay, some of you are already doubting whether or not this really works. So, give it a try...you'll see that I really am true to My Word."

Malachi 3:10

"Bring the whole tithe into the storehouse, that there may be food in my house. Test me in this," says the LORD Almighty, "and see if I will not throw open the floodgates of heaven and pour out so much blessing that you will not have room enough for it."

HOW OLD SHOULD MY CHILDREN BE BEFORE THEY START TITHING?

Parents should teach their children to tithe as soon as they are old enough to understand what giving is all about. They need to understand at an early age the importance of obeying and applying biblical principles.

Proverbs 22:6

Train a child in the way he should go, and when he is old he will not turn from it.

DO I GIVE 10 PERCENT ON MY GROSS INCOME OR NET INCOME?

Our tithe is always on our increase. You should think even beyond the monetary value of your paycheck. First of all, according to Exodus 23:16, 19, we are to give of our firstfruits. Proverbs 3:9 encourages us to honor the Lord with our wealth and the firstfruits of our crops. Growing up in my father's home, tithing meant our money, our garden, our bonus, our time, etc. Think aggregate, cumulative, the total, the whole, etc.

I AM ON A FIXED INCOME.

It comes down to this: Are you going to trust the promises of God that you will never be in want, or will your trust be only in yourself? Trust God and see how supernatural provision will be yours.

What are the benefits of tithing?

The ministries of the church are funded. The vision of the church is fulfilled. The poor and needy are helped. Since God loves a cheerful giver, we experience the love of God like never before. He blesses our family life both spiritually and financially in ways that could not be experienced before. We experience God's response to our obedience. Tithing triggers the Malachi 3:10–11 test—open heavens and showers of blessings. By stepping out in faith, we enter a whole new realm in the Spirit world. When we walk by faith, we open the door of opportunity to see miracles happen in our life.

What does it mean to "rebuke the devourer"?

Malachi 3:10–11

Bring ye all the tithes into the storehouse, that there may be meat in mine house, and prove me now herewith, saith the LORD of hosts, if I will not open you the windows of heaven, and pour you out a blessing, that there shall not be room enough to receive it. And I will rebuke the devourer for your sakes, and he shall not destroy the fruits of your ground; neither shall your vine cast her fruit before the time in the field, saith the LORD of hosts. (KJV)

The tithe (the first tenth) does not belong to you. It belongs to God. Many things come against us in our financial life. It may be the loss of a job, auto repair expenses, house maintenance, appliance breakdown, or health-care related expenses. From time to time, we all can acknowledge some difficulty in these areas. And when out-of-nowhere expenses come, they can be burdensome and costly. However, what we don't know is all that God keeps *away* from us. When we are faithful in our giving, the Word states simply that our crops will be large and that He will keep the insects and plagues away. Whether you are a farmer, a tiller of the ground, or simply planting crops of a nonagricultural nature, you can rest assured that God is working on your behalf.

SHOULD I BE GIVING ABOVE MY TITHE?

Yes. You should give offerings as you become aware of need, to support vision, aid in missions at home and abroad, and give to any other areas that the Holy Spirit prompts you.

Luke 6:38

"Give, and it will be given to you. A good measure, pressed down, shaken together and running over, will be poured into your lap. For with the measure you use, it will be measured to you."

Acts 20:35

In everything I did, I showed you that by this kind of hard work we must help the weak, remembering the words the Lord Jesus himself said: "It is more blessed to give than to receive."

It is the very nature of God to give. He gave of Himself. He loves the opportunity to give gifts to His children. When we give, gifts are given to us. Giving is often the result of our ability and desire to respond to specific needs. Sometimes giving is an act of faith on our part. When we move into faith giving, it is the very nature of God to respond in much the same way.

I PAY MY TITHES REGULARLY, WITH CONSISTENCY AND ACCURACY. BUT HOW MANY AND HOW MUCH SHOULD I GIVE IN OFFERINGS?

2 Corinthians 9:6

Remember this: Whoever sows sparingly will also reap sparingly, and whoever sows generously will also reap generously.

CHAPTER 4

Tithing In Scripture

Genesis 14:18–20

Then Melchizedek king of Salem brought out bread and wine; he was the priest of God Most High. And he blessed him and said: "Blessed be Abram of God Most High, Possessor of heaven and earth; And blessed be God Most High, Who has delivered your enemies into your hand." And he gave him a tithe of all.

Leviticus 27:30-32

And all the tithe of the land, whether of the seed of the land or of the fruit of the tree, is the LORD's. It is holy to the LORD. If a man wants at all to redeem any of his tithes, he shall add one-fifth to it. And concerning the tithe of the herd or the flock, of whatever passes under the rod, the tenth one shall be holy to the LORD.

Numbers 18:21

Behold, I have given the children of Levi all the tithes in Israel as an inheritance in return for the work which they perform, the work of the tabernacle of meeting.

Numbers 18:24–28

"For the tithes of the children of Israel, which they offer up as a heave offering to the LORD, I have given to the Levites as an inheritance; therefore I have said to them, 'Among the children of Israel they shall have no inheritance.'"

Then the LORD spoke to Moses, saying, "Speak thus to the Levites, and say to them: 'When you take from the children of Israel the tithes which I have given you from them as your inheritance, then you shall offer up a heave offering of it to the LORD, a tenth of the tithe.' Thus you shall also offer a heave offering to the LORD from all your tithes which you receive from the children of Israel, and you shall give the LORD's heave offering from it to Aaron the priest."

Deuteronomy 12:6

There you shall take your burnt offerings, your sacrifices, your tithes, the heave offerings of your hand, your vowed offerings, your freewill offerings, and the firstborn of your herds and flocks.

Deuteronomy 12:11

Then there will be the place where the LORD your God chooses to make His name abide. There you shall bring all that I command you: your burnt offerings, your sacrifices, your tithes, the heave offerings of your hand, and all your choice offerings which you vow to the LORD.

Deuteronomy 12:17

You may not eat within your gates the tithe of your grain or your new wine or your oil, of the firstlings of your herd or your flock, of any of your offerings which you vow, of your freewill offerings, or of the heave offering of your hand.

Deuteronomy 14:22-23

You shall truly tithe all the increase of your grain that the field produces year by year. And you shall eat before the LORD your God, in the place where He chooses to make His name abide, the tithe of your grain and your new wine and your oil, of the firstborn of your herds and your flocks, that you may learn to fear the LORD your God always.

Deuteronomy 14:28

At the end of every third year you shall bring out the tithe of your produce of that year and store it up within your gates.

Deuteronomy 26:12

When you have finished laying aside all the tithe of your increase in the third year — the year of tithing — and have given it to the Levite, the stranger, the fatherless, and the widow, so that they may eat within your gates and be filled,

2 Chronicles 31:5

As soon as the commandment was circulated, the children of Israel brought in abundance the firstfruits of grain and wine, oil and honey, and of all the produce of the field; and they brought in abundantly the tithe of everything.

2 Chronicles 31:12

Then they faithfully brought in the offerings, the tithes, and the dedicated things; Cononiah the Levite had charge of them, and Shimei his brother was the next.

Nehemiah 10:37-38

To bring the firstfruits of our dough, our offerings, the fruit from all kinds of trees, the new wine and oil, to the priests, to the storerooms of the house of our God; and to bring the tithes of our land to the Levites, for the Levites should receive the tithes in all our farming communities. And the priest, the descendant of Aaron, shall be with the Levites when the Levites receive tithes; and the Levites shall bring up a tenth of the tithes to the house of our God, to the rooms of the storehouse.

Nehemiah 12:44

And at the same time some were appointed over the rooms of the storehouse for the offerings, the firstfruits, and the tithes, to gather into them from the fields of the cities the portions specified by the Law for the priests and Levites; for Judah rejoiced over the priests and Levites who ministered.

Nehemiah 13:5

And he had prepared for him a large room, where previously they had stored the grain offerings, the frankincense, the articles, the tithes of grain, the new wine and oil, which were commanded to be given to the Levites and singers and gatekeepers, and the offerings for the priests.

Nehemiah 13:12

Then all Judah brought the tithe of the grain and the new wine and the oil to the storehouse.

Amos 4:4

Come to Bethel and transgress, at Gilgal multiply transgression; bring your sacrifices every morning, your tithes every three days.

Malachi 3:8

Will a man rob God? Yet you have robbed Me! But you say, "In what way have we robbed You?" In tithes and offerings.

Malachi 3:10

"Bring all the tithes into the storehouse, that there may be food in My house, and try Me now in this," says the LORD of hosts, "If I will not open for you the windows of heaven and pour out for you such blessing that there will not be room enough to receive it."

Matthew 23:23

"Woe to you, scribes and Pharisees, hypocrites! For you pay tithe of mint and anise and cummin, and have neglected the weightier matters of the law: justice and mercy and faith. These you ought to have done, without leaving the others undone."

Luke 11:42

"But woe to you Pharisees! For you tithe mint and rue and all manner of herbs, and pass by justice and the love of God. These you ought to have done, without leaving the others undone."

Luke 18:12

"I fast twice a week; I give tithes of all that I possess."

Hebrews 7:5-6

And indeed those who are of the sons of Levi, who receive the priesthood, have a commandment to receive tithes from the people according to the law, that is, from their brethren, though they have come from the loins of Abraham; But he whose genealogy is not derived from them received tithes from Abraham and blessed him who had the promises.

Hebrews 7:8-9

Here mortal men receive tithes, but there he receives them, of whom it is witnessed that he lives. Even Levi, who receives tithes, paid tithes through Abraham, so to speak.

SEGMENT TWO

The Blessing of Giving

Giving to others brings indescribable pleasure. An inward joy comes to you when you have reached out and helped others. Whether it be in monetary gifts or simply rolling up your sleeves and helping out the old-fashioned way, the act of giving brings its own reward. When you give first, your own personal needs will be automatically taken care of. After all, giving is the Lord's work. It is Christianity in action. Jesus Christ had something to say about giving to others.

Matthew 25:35–40

"For I was hungry and you gave me something to eat, I was thirsty and you gave me something to drink, I was a stranger and you invited me in, I needed clothes and you clothed me, I was sick and you looked after me, I was in prison and you came to visit me." Then the righteous will answer him, "Lord, when did we see you hungry and feed you, or thirsty and give you

something to drink? When did we see you a stranger and invite you in, or needing clothes and clothe you? When did we see you sick or in prison and go to visit you?" The King will reply, "I tell you the truth, whatever you did for one of the least of these brothers of mine, you did for me."

In the verses, Jesus was not just speaking about seasonal giving. Of course, during the holiday season of Thanksgiving and Christmas, many of us tend to think more often about giving to others. Some people think of giving only around these holidays. It is pleasant to give gifts to children and family, but how much more desirable is it to give gifts to someone who cannot return the favor, to someone who is not expecting anything from you? What about your giving the other eleven months of the year? How can you be a giver during that time? ∞

CHAPTER 5

The Blessing of Giving Generously

Many Scriptures in the Bible talk about giving. They instruct us how to give, when to give, where to give, why we give, and what to give. All these verses are not meant to bring us down, point a finger in our face, or discourage us. They are there to bring us happiness, merriment, and a sense of well-being! It is wonderful to be a giver in every sense of the word! The unhappy people in life are those who keep everything for themselves. They are the discontented ones who are selfish, living life only to please themselves and chase after their own personal wants.

Giving is fun! Giving is exciting! Just try to give something away without feeling wonderful. The non-giver is a very miserable individual. When you are feeling blue and discouraged, try giving of yourself to others. Give away something and discover what you receive in return. You will receive happiness, hope, a sense of peace and well-being, and instant encouragement will come your way. Give even to your enemies. Drive them absolutely crazy with your selflessness and love.

BE A GOOD STEWARD

Stewardship is a biblical requirement for all Christians. It is all about blessing others, giving to others, and practicing the art of putting good intentions to action.

Matthew 25:21

"His master replied, 'Well done, good and faithful servant! You have been faithful with a few things; I will put you in charge of many things. Come and share your master's happiness!'"

The Bible is clear that our position in regard to property is as stewards, not owners. A steward is a guardian of the interests of another. The steward owns nothing, but carefully guards, protects, and increases the property of the One he serves. The essential quality of a steward is faithfulness. When we are faithful, God gives us more because we have proven we are diligent to use what He gives us wisely and generously.

1 Chronicles 29:11–14

"Yours, O LORD, is the greatness and the power and the glory and the majesty and the splendor, for everything in heaven and earth is yours. Yours, O LORD, is the kingdom; you are exalted as head over all. Wealth and honor come from you; you are the ruler of all things. In your hands are strength and power to exalt and give strength to all. Now, our God, we give you thanks, and praise your glorious name. But who am I, and who are my people, that we should be able to give as generously as this? Everything comes from you, and we have given you only what comes from your hand."

This prayer of David reflects the heart of a humble steward. He acknowledges that everything in heaven and earth belongs to God. He recognizes God as the head and ruler of everything, the giver of wealth and honor. God gives us things we may use, but ultimately everything belongs to God. The steward understands total dependence on God and gives generously to the Lord, simply from understanding that everything comes from Him.

GIVE YOUR TIME

Your personal time is very valuable. We know that. In our busy world of work, children, family, school, church, and the like, our time might be the hardest thing to give. Yet it is probably the most precious commodity we have. After all, our time on earth is short lived, and we have only so much allotted to us. What we don't use wisely is gone forever. When you give your time to others, they value it strongly. One of God's greatest gifts is time. Time is our tool. It is a wonderful gift. You can give this gift to others. Here are some examples of how you can give your time to others.

- Clean up litter in a neighborhood park.

- Take your family to a church maintenance day.

- Serve your church as greeters, ushers, teachers, filing clerks, visitor follow-up, etc.

- Gather and collect household items for the poor and needy.

- Clean an area of the church, either inside or outside.

- Bake a pie and deliver to your local firemen.

- Mow the grass of an elderly person.

- Visit the sick and incarcerated.

- Volunteer at a soup kitchen.

- Change the oil in the vehicle of a person who has been ill.

- Bake cookies or bread and take them to a shut-in or elderly person.

- Fix broken toys for children.

- Provide child care for a single mother.

- Gather coats in the fall and distribute to needy families.

- Befriend a lonely person.

- Rake a neighbor's leaves in the fall.

- Prune rosebushes, plant flowers, and help older people.

- Write a thank-you note and send to your neighborhood police or fire station.

The list of what you can do with your time in service to others is endless. When you give to others, you make a difference in their lives. Often you give them hope and encouragement they cannot find anywhere else. One should always have an attitude of service. This means being aware and anticipating the needs of someone else. This means offering to help instead of waiting to be asked. You serve God by helping others. God is always giving to us continually. We can express His love to others by showing them genuine generosity.

GIVE YOUR MONEY

Exodus 35:5

From what you have, take an offering for the LORD. Everyone who is willing is to bring to the LORD an offering of gold, silver and bronze...

This verse advises us that a willing heart is a must for giving offerings. God gave us a free will so we would love Him voluntarily. The same applies to our offerings. He doesn't demand that we give more than the tithe, but when we give of our free will, we are telling Him that we love Him and that our desire is to worship Him with our offerings.

It is required that you give God the tenth of your increase that already belongs to Him, and it is always in our best interest to give above and beyond in offerings and designated gifts. How else can we be involved in giving? I offer the following suggestions to consider in your giving perspective:

- Give to an overseas missions project.

- Give toward feeding the poor in your city.

- Give to help an unemployed family with their house payment.

- Give to a worthy charity.

Endless special projects and numerous charities could use your financial support. So how does one determine to whom to donate hard-earned money? We cannot help all the world, but we can help those with whom we are closest and those whom we have become aware of. Of course, we can love the world or help some overseas mission project, but can we love and help our neighbor? What kind of special needs do you have in your own neighborhood?

GIVE YOUR RESOURCES

A Mayan woman in Belize, Central America, desired to give a gift to the missionary who had brought her the gospel. She knew the missionary's greatest need was money, though she had none to give, for they did not use money in her village. She did not have livestock to give that could be eaten or even an extra portion of vegetables for the missionary to enjoy. All she had was the skill of her hands. She made a living by weaving intricate tapestry—it took her forty hours a week for an entire month to produce just one tapestry. She decided she would work twice as much to produce an extra carpet to give. This offering blessed the missionary's heart more than any sum of money could have because it represented the woman's time, her skill, and her heart.

Perhaps you do not have money to give. You can honor the Lord by offering your time and your skill. What are your skills? Are you good at typing? What about volunteering at the church office? Are you good at reading aloud to children? What about volunteering for story time in your church's children's ministry? Your church will probably be very blessed by the offering of your time and skill. There is always a way to give an offering—no matter how tight things are financially—so give with your heart.

Everyone has resources for giving. No, I am not talking about money, nor am I necessarily referring to time, though it could involve our time. I am speaking of those things that can be given for a specific purpose or at a specific time. What if you are a professional nurse and you know of an elderly person who could use a medical visit from time to time? You can give the gift of your vocation to those you know. Perhaps you are a carpenter, and a single mom's porch is badly in need of repairs. Maybe you are a landscaper, and you could lend a hand to a disabled household. Maybe you own a truck, and a poor family needs a helping hand in moving to a new home. You may be a whiz at science or math, and a young neighbor needs some extra tutoring. Get creative in giving your personal resources.

Give Yourself

We, as the body of Christ, are responsible for the health and welfare of all the parts of the body. We are also responsible for reflecting the heart of Christ to those in need in our society. One of the most important ways we can give an offering to God, as revealed by the following passage, is by meeting a need. Check your local church to find out if you might be able to meet any needs.

Hebrews 13:16

And do not forget to do good and to share with others, for with such sacrifices God is pleased.

Give Because God Is Good

Matthew 12:35

"The good man brings good things out of the good stored up in him, and the evil man brings evil things out of the evil stored up in him."

When our hearts are filled with the goodness of God, we will give from that goodness. Let's allow our hearts to be filled with the following truths about God's goodness.

- God wants to bless your work. (Deuteronomy 28:12)
- God wants to make your work increase and prosper. (Deuteronomy 30:9)
- God will keep His promises to you. (Joshua 21:45)
- The Lord's mercy endures forever. (Ezra 3:11)
- The Lord wants to put His good hand upon you. (Nehemiah 2:8)
- God is good and upright. (Psalm 25:8; 34:8; 100:5)
- God does that which is good. (Psalm 119:68)
- God wants to show you His lovingkindness. (Psalm 69:16)
- God is good to the pure in heart. (Psalm 73:1)
- God wants to give every good thing to you. (Psalm 84:11)
- God wants to give you good things and increase your business. (Psalm 85:12)
- God will be abundant in mercy toward you. (Psalm 86:5)
- God wants to give good gifts to you. (Matthew 7:11)

To give is to yield control or possession of something, surrendering it. It is to yield oneself and one's possessions without restraint or control. Giving is bestowing, conferring, imparting, granting — it's delivering something. In short, it is to put something into the possession of another for his use. When we give to God, we are yielding control of our possessions to Him and allowing Him to use them as He sees fit.

We have already discussed the giving of the tithe, a tenth of all our increase, but what does it mean to give an offering? An offering is an undesignated, unlimited amount given as a freewill love gift unto the Lord. We are encouraged in Scripture to grow in the grace of giving. The tithe remains, but giving offerings provide us with the opportunity to grow in liberality, generosity, faith, and service. When you give with joy and give with all your heart, you are not concerned so much with giving an amount of minimal acceptance. Instead, you give with a heart that desires that all of your resources be used for God's glory.

One man of great faith who was used to bless a nation was George Muller. He said this:

> The child of God must be willing to be a channel through which God's abundant blessings flow. This channel may be narrow and shallow at first, yet some of the waters of God's bounty can pass through. If we cheerfully yield ourselves to this purpose, the channel becomes wider and deeper, allowing more of the bounty of God to pass through. We cannot limit the extent to which God may use us as instruments in communicating blessing if we are willing to yield ourselves to Him and are careful to give Him all the glory.[4]

Deuteronomy 28:12

> The LORD will open the heavens, the storehouse of his bounty, to send rain on your land in season and to bless all the work of your hands. You will lend to many nations but will borrow from none.

"If a person gets his attitude towards money straight, it will help straighten out almostt every other area of his life. Tell me what you think about money, and I can tell you what you think about God, for these two are closely related. A man's heart is closer to his wallet than almost anything else." —Billy Graham

GIVING ON A LIMITED BUDGET

Financial bondage caused by past ignorance of principles or by mishandling of funds must be taken care of before you can live a life of abundant giving. People with serious financial problems may not be financially free to give offerings. Those who have lived a life of poor money management must come into a place of financial freedom so they can become channels of God's money. Financial freedom comes when we live according to the attitude that our resources are to be used to serve God, His church, and others, not just to comfort ourselves. Living according to this attitude requires a decision, but more than that, it is a discipline that must be developed. Coming in to this place of financial freedom should be a priority for you if you fit into this category. However, that does not mean that you cannot begin to cultivate a desire and heart for giving now. Sometimes giving can be outside of the realm of finances.

Exodus 35:24–26

Those presenting an offering of silver or bronze brought it as an offering to the Lord, and everyone who had acacia wood for any part of the work brought it. Every skilled woman spun with her hands and brought what she had spun—blue, purple or scarlet yarn or fine linen. And all the women who were willing and had the skill spun the goat hair.

They may not have had silver or bronze or other such earthly treasures, but these industrious women of the Old Testament desired to give an offering of their own. They gave an offering to the Lord of their skill and of their time.

Perhaps you do not have money to give. You can honor the Lord by offering your time and your skill. What are your skills? Are you good at typing? What about volunteering at the church office? Are you good at reading aloud to children? What about volunteering for story time in your church's children's ministry? Your church will probably be very blessed by the offering of your time and skill. There is always a way to give an offering—no matter how tight things are financially—so let's give with our hearts.

1 Kings 17:8–16

Then the word of the LORD came to him: "Go at once to Za-rephath of Sidon and stay there. I have commanded a widow in

that place to supply you with food." So he went to Zarephath.
When he came to the town gate, a widow was there gathering
sticks. He called to her and asked, "Would you bring me a little
water in a jar so I may have a drink?" As she was going to
get it, he called, "And bring me, please, a piece of bread." "As
surely as the LORD your God lives," she replied, "I don't have
any bread — only a handful of flour in a jar and a little oil in a
jug. I am gathering a few sticks to take home and make a meal
for myself and my son, that we may eat it—and die." Elijah
said to her, "Don't be afraid. Go home and do as you have said.
But first make a small cake of bread for me from what you have
and bring it to me, and then make something for yourself and
your son. For this is what the LORD, the God of Israel, says:
The jar of flour will not be used up and the jug of oil will not
run dry until the day the LORD gives rain on the land."

She went away and did as Elijah had told her. So there was food
every day for Elijah and for the woman and her family. For the jar
of flour was not used up and the jug of oil did not run dry, in keeping with the word of the LORD spoken by Elijah.

This story is about a woman who gave to God in faith and obedience to meet the need of another with what she had in her household. Elijah was dependent on God's provision through this poor
widow, one who had almost nothing and was ready to die. This
woman was in a famine, a time to be very careful and self-protect-
ing. But the famine was not in her spirit. She had a generous and
giving spirit. The famine could not break her; her generosity could
not be bound. She gave out of her need and poverty from what she
had in her household.

This story shows that even if you feel that you are lacking, God
can use the things you do have to meet a need. You may feel that
you just don't have the money to give right now to that orphanage
in Africa. What do you have in your household that God can use,
like the flour and oil the widow had in her household? Maybe it's
that bag of toys sitting in the garage that will be the perfect thing
for the orphanage.

If you cannot afford to give largely, you must not despise the day of small beginnings. God never asks us to give what we do not have; He only asks that we be willing to give all that we do have. Second Corinthians 8:12 shows us that it is the heart that matters: "For if the willingness is there, the gift is acceptable according to what one has, not according to what he does not have." We can look to the needs and then look to our own household, listening to and obeying the voice of the Holy Spirit when He says, "Give.'"

Like this widow, we too will experience seasons of testing. Enduring such seasons will teach us faith and trust in God. We must not allow a spirit of poverty to bind us, choke us, or keep us from giving. If you are experiencing a season like this right now, I encourage you to take the words of Elijah to heart. In 1 Kings 17:13, he tells the widow, "Do not be afraid." When in doubt, we must believe the words of hope that fill the Scriptures, not fearing what our minds or circumstances may say to us. As we put fear aside, we move into the realm of faith, trusting God to provide for us just as He did the widow of Zarephath.

Generosity Is God's Antidote to Greed.

The heart and attitude of a blessed person is worth looking at. After all, doesn't everyone want to be a "blessed person"? Blessed people are set apart in many ways because they have learned how to be blessed. We all have the opportunity to receive the blessing of God and be "under the shadow of the Almighty" if we so desire. The blessed person gives of his or her resources freely, cheerfully, and out of genuine appreciation to God.

We Gain by Giving. We Lose by Withholding.

What about the heart of a blessed person? What theme was so important to Jesus that He talked about it more than anything else? Was it heaven? Was it repentance? Was it prayer? Was it salvation? No to each of the preceding. It was the subject of money. *He must have known that if He had our money, He would certainly have our hearts.* According to the values of the world, we are to earn money, take pleasure in our money, overspend on self-indulgence, repay our debt with interest, save for retirement if we have run out of toys to purchase, and then consider an occasional annual gift to charity to make us feel good. The Bible's way is much different:

- We are to work hard to earn money.

- We are to tithe and give offerings.

- We are to save in order to take care of our family now and in the future.

- We are to repay everything owed.

- We are to enjoy whatever God has loaned to us and allowed us to receive.

What about the attitude of a blessed person? Overall the principle attitude must be that all money and all possessions belong to God. He trusts us with the care of these things until we prove ourselves unworthy of His trust. Since it is not our money, it's not our problem to worry about it. It is our fiduciary responsibility as good stewards to use it correctly. Since God does not need our money, He must be more interested in growing our faith—growing our trust in Him.

GENEROUS GIVING

2 Corinthians 8:2

Out of the most severe trial, their overflowing joy and their extreme poverty welled up in rich generosity.

Giving generously is expected of all Christians. After all, we have freely received much—forgiveness of sins, salvation, relationship with God...and the list goes on. In the book of beginnings, Jacob made his commitment to giving known:

Genesis 28:20–22

Then Jacob made a vow, saying, "If God will be with me and will watch over me on this journey I am taking and will give

*me food to eat and clothes to wear so that I return safely to my
father's house, then the LORD will be my God and this stone
that I have set up as a pillar will be God's house, and of all that
you give me I will give you a tenth."*

Early in biblical history, we see a picture of Jacob, a man who
promised God he would return a tenth of all his increase. Jacob was
beginning a journey, apparently leaving his family for a period of
time, making his bed under the stars. God came to Jacob in a dream,
promising him great blessings in the future, which He, of course,
fulfilled. Jacob promised a tenth, as he understood the principle of
giving.

Luke 6:38

*"Give, and it shall be given unto you; good measure, pressed
down, and shaken together, and running over, shall men give
into your bosom. For the measure you give will be the measure
you get back." (KJV)*

Giving is God's trigger for financial miracles. We gain by giving. When you give to the kingdom of God, it will be given back
to you. But where will it come from? Who will give to you? Will
God cause money to float down from the heavenlies so your needs
are met? No, the second part of verse 38 says, "shall men give into
your...[life]" (KJV). This is how the cycle of blessing works: *When
you give to God, God in turn causes others to give to you,* which could
be in the form of new customers to your business, new products to
sell, and so on. When God owns your business, He will make sure
it prospers! Nothing happens in the economy of God until you give
something away. It is a universal law of God. Paul very appropriately reminds us:

2 Corinthians 9:6–9

*Remember this: Whoever sows sparingly will also reap spar-
ingly, and whoever sows generously will also reap generously.
Each man should give what he has decided in his heart to give,*

not reluctantly or under compulsion, for God loves a cheerful giver. And God is able to make all grace abound to you, so that in all things at all times, having all that you need, you will abound in every good work.

Giving begins with tithing. Tithing is all about obedience. Tithing has everything to do with trusting God and His promises. Tithing is done in faith. We tithe because He says to. We tithe because we trust Him. Our act of faith brings results. Disobedience is a serious matter. God had a great future planned for King Saul. He wanted to bless his life and fill it with great authority, power, and riches. But then Saul chose to disobey.

1 Samuel 15:19

Why did you not obey the LORD? Why did you pounce on the plunder and do evil in the eyes of the LORD?

1 Samuel 15:23

For rebellion is like the sin of divination, and arrogance like the evil of idolatry. Because you have rejected the word of the LORD, He has rejected you as king.

1 Samuel 15:25–26

"Now I beg you, forgive my sin and come back with me, so that I may worship the LORD." But Samuel said to him, "I will not go back with you. You have rejected the word of the LORD, and the LORD has rejected you as king over Israel!"

Saul was rejected as king of Israel because of his disobedience. Everything God had planned for Saul was given to David. Be careful that you do not keep what belongs to God.

GIVING BEFORE GETTING

2 Corinthians 8:7

But just as you excel in everything—in faith, in speech, in knowledge, in complete earnestness and in your love for us— see that you also excel in this grace of giving.

Is having a lot of money the key to everything? Does money bring happiness? Does money bring solutions to life's problems? If you had a limitless amount of money and could buy anything you wanted, what would you buy? When would you stop buying, gathering, grasping, and grabbing? Our wealth does not come from what we accumulate in life, but from what we give in life.

Some of the wealthiest men in the world gathered in 1923 at the Edgewater Beach Hotel in Chicago. This group of seven was worth more than the entire U.S. Treasury in their time. These were great financial men with records of success who had achieved great prosperity.

But this was not the end of their story. Within twenty-five years the president of the largest steel company had died penniless. A millionaire wheat speculator had also become poor. Another, who was the president of the New York Stock Exchange, had already spent many years in prison. Yet another of the wealthy seven who was a member of the president's cabinet had spent time in prison, but was pardoned so he could die at home instead of prison. The fifth of the seven committed suicide; the sixth man, who headed one of the world's largest companies, also took his own life. The seventh and last of the world's richest men also took his own life.

Acts 20:35

Remembering the words the Lord Jesus himself said: "It is more blessed to give than to receive."

Luke 6:38

> "Give, and it will be given to you. A good measure, pressed
> down, shaken together and running over, will be poured into
> your lap. For with the measure you use, it will be measured to
> you."

Mother Teresa was a woman of God who never stopped giving of herself. She said, "Never worry about numbers. Help one person at a time, and always start with the person nearest you."

GIVING IN GRACE

True givers are not motivated by competition; they are motivated by grace. What is this grace? In 2 Corinthians 8 and 9, it is referred to as a divine favor that is displayed in generosity. It is the divine enablement to participate greatly in giving. An act of grace as used in this passage means an act of giving. Grace causes pleasure and is delightful; it means to be regarded favorably; it is a mercy that causes joy.

Grace is that which makes one ready, quick, and willing to give freely. Grace dignifies and lifts people up in its gift of favor; it honors and blesses and supplies all that is needed. Grace is the initiator of giving. Neither biblical law, a set of rules, nor guilt or competition should make you give. It is grace that creates the desire to give, grace that gives us the ability to give, and grace that causes us to move into the realm of faith. Second Corinthians 8:6–7 says that giving is something we need to excel and abound in, but it must be motivated by grace.

CHEERFUL GIVING

1 Chronicles 29:9

> Then the people rejoiced, for they had offered willingly, because
> with a loyal heart they had offered willingly to the LORD; and
> King David also rejoiced greatly. (NKJV)

Giving should never be burdensome. It should never be stressful. Our gifts should not be presented in doubt or clothed in reluctance or reservation. In fact, giving as seen in this passage should be an occasion for great joy! Our gifts should be presented in faith, presenting them to God with confidence in His Word. If we give with a grudging spirit and attitude, does it hinder God from giving us full blessing? I don't know. But what I do know is that God just simply loves one who gives cheerfully and wholeheartedly.

2 Corinthians 9:7

> *Each man should give what he has decided in his heart to give, not reluctantly or under compulsion, for God loves a cheerful giver.*

In this verse it is clear that giving (we are not talking about returning God's tenth to Him) should not be coerced. No one should be intimidated into giving. No one should be pressured into giving. Giving must not be compulsory or motivated by guilt; it is to be exercised out of one's free will and love.

Giving is a personal decision to bless others as God has blessed us. We do this through supporting the various ministries of our local church. Yes, there are other giving opportunities, but be careful to first sustain the place where you are fed week in and week out. Take care to give willingly and cheerfully.

HOW SHOULD I GIVE TO THE WORK OF GOD?

Many churches offer opportunities to give to the Lord in a variety of ways. Check with your church for an avenue to give:

- To the poor.
- To the needs of children.
- Toward retiring any debt the church has.
- Toward new churches being planted.
- Toward strategic, creative evangelism.

- Toward constructing new buildings to be used for the purposes of God.

- Toward Christian education (schools and colleges).

- Toward the needs of the community (pregnancy centers, counseling, child abuse centers).

- Toward the purchase of necessary equipment for your church.

- Toward capital improvements for the church.

- In the inheritance you will leave behind.

Beyond the needs and special giving projects of your local church and community, one way to give to the work of God is by giving to your church an offering designated for use in world missions. This is one way to reach out to the world, because not all of us can go to the mission field, but we can all help someone else go. According to the "Status of Global Mission, in context of 20th and 21st centuries," the personal income of American church members combined is $15,198 billion per year, whereas the worldwide total given to missions is $15 billion, less than one-thousandth. For every dollar to missions, we spend six hundred dollars on luxuries. We can do more, and this work needs to be done.

John Wesley donated to mission causes by sacrificing personal comforts. Living simply, he was able to give more than five hundred thousand dollars to missions in his lifetime. When asked about this personal sacrifice, his answer was, "Gladly would I again make the floor my bed, a box my chair, a box my table, rather than that men should perish for want of the knowledge of the Savior."

We too can have an impact like John Wesley. It is certainly worth considering making a plan to give to missions. Some families may have a goal of giving in specific-dollar increments on a regular basis, though some families may be challenged to give more. For most families, such a goal is doable and can make a difference in missions. Setting reasonable giving goals will help you to be consistent and faithful and help you not forget to give to missions. You may consider evaluating your finances and making a commitment to yourself and to the Lord for one year of missions giving. Even if you start small, small is better than nothing! Every year, you should consider reevaluating your missions giving commitment to see if the Lord is asking you to give more.

During the Second World War, Winston Churchill, then prime minister of Great Britain, set out to "win with words" over Hitler by raising the morale of the nation. Not only did he visit the troops and factories, but he also went to the out-of-the-way coal-mining towns. On one visit to the hardworking coal miners, the prime minister urged them to see their significance in the total effort for victory. He told them:

"We will be victorious! We will preserve our freedom. And years from now when our freedom is secure and peace reigns, your children and children's children will come and they will say to you, 'What did you do to win our freedom in that great war?' And one will say, 'I marched with the Eighth Army!' Someone else will proudly say, 'I manned a submarine.' And another will say, 'I guided the ships that moved the troops and supplies.' And still another will say, 'I doctored the wounds!'"

Then the great statesman paused. The dirty-faced miners sat in silence and awe, waiting for him to proceed. "They will come to you," he shouted, "and you will say, with equal right and equal pride, 'I cut the coal! I cut the coal that fueled the ships that moved the supplies! That's what I did. I cut the coal!'"

We can all do our part. Maybe we are not on the frontlines, just like the coal miners in this story. However we can supply the fuel for these efforts. Our part is just as necessary as that person overseas, so let us partner together to fund God's kingdom.

GIVING FREELY

Matthew 10:8

"Freely you have received, freely give."

God expects us to be generous and also to give with balance. David wrote in Psalm 112:5, 9: "Good will come to him who is generous.... He has scattered abroad his gifts to the poor, his righteousness endures forever; his horn will be lifted high in honor." The true spirit and attitude of giving (helping the needy) is at the heart of Jesus' instruction in the Sermon on the Mount. In Luke 6:35, we are told not to expect a lot in return for our kindness, "...without expecting to get anything back. Then your reward will be great."

So should we then give just in order to get? Absolutely not! A giving person gives out of a spirit of genuine generosity. When he or she receives, it is a totally unexpected blessing. Seeking to get is disastrous to the spirit of giving! Remember it was Jesus Christ, Son of Man, Son of God, who said, "It is more blessed to give than to receive" (Acts 20:35, KJV).

Generosity is God's antidote to greed. We gain by giving. We lose by withholding. The person who wants blessing upon life is one who understands giving generously. Why is it more blessed to give than to receive? When we give freely and generously, we put God first, and ahead of our own selfish interests. By doing this, we are obeying His Word and this obedience will cause Him to bless us. When we give freely and generously, this shows that we trust God. The degree of our giving is a clear indication of our freedom from fear. Freedom from fear is always a blessing.

Freely giving protects us from the pitfalls of greed and materialism. Generous giving comes from a humble, loving heart. Greed and selfishness are derived from a prideful "me first" attitude, and this serves to put barriers between us and the blessings of God. First Peter 5:5 says, "God resisteth the proud, and giveth grace to the humble" (KJV).

Our giving must be bountiful and with the knowledge that our kindness and generosity will ultimately be of much help to those in need. It is not the amount of our gift, but it is our motive behind the gift. We are not to give grudgingly or out of necessity or sorrow. Don't give large gifts if you feel obliged to do so. Don't give sorrowfully because you are giving out of regard for public opinion. Give out of a sense of need and a pure motive. This is the kind of giving in which God delights—giving cheerfully, with laughter, delight, exuberance, and joyfulness. When we manage to grasp these principles, giving really does become a blessing. "Each one must do just as he has purposed in his heart, not grudgingly or under compulsion, for God loves a cheerful giver" (2 Corinthians 9:7, NASB).

We have been blessed beyond measure, and now it is time to return the blessing. This verse simply infers a spirit of liberality. And yet like the gospel message, it is so simple that men and women stumble over its simplicity—freely you have received, so you should freely give.

Giving Gifts

2 Corinthians 9:9

He has scattered abroad his gifts to the poor; his righteousness endures forever.

Giving to the Needy

1 John 3:17

If anyone has material possessions and sees his brother in need but has no pity on him, how can the love of God be in him.

If our attitude is one of hoarding what we have, God will stop giving to us. If we are ever going to be financially free, we must allow God to use us as a conduit in which to bless others. The needs of others must be met by our generous giving. If we are open and generous with the things He has provided us, God will bless us in a great way.

Christians must understand that the lesson of stewardship is found in returning to God all that He has provided and entrusted to our care. Failure to give back to God what He has generously given to us is to be condemned. Maturing in Christ means developing a growing spirit of generosity and a willingness to share.

Giving out of Your Poverty

2 Corinthians 8:1–5

Out of the most severe trial, their overflowing joy and their extreme poverty welled up in rich generosity. For I testify that they gave as much as they were able, and even beyond their ability. Entirely on their own, they urgently pleaded with us for the privilege of sharing in this service to the saints.

Giving Special Gifts

Deuteronomy 12:11-12

Then to the place the LORD your God will choose as a dwelling for his Name—there you are to bring everything I command you: your burnt offerings and sacrifices, your tithes and special gifts, and all the choice possessions you have vowed to the LORD.

Sacrificial Giving

Luke 21:4

"All these people gave their gifts out of their wealth; but she out of her poverty put in all she had to live on.

Mark 12:41–44"

Jesus sat down opposite the place where the offerings were put and watched the crowd putting their money into the temple treasury. Many rich people threw in large amounts. But a poor widow came and put in two very small copper coins, worth only a fraction of a penny. Calling his disciples to him, Jesus said, "I tell you the truth, this poor widow has put more into the treasury than all the others. They all gave out of their wealth; but she, out of her poverty, put in everything—all she had to live on."

Most definitely you need God to be involved in your financial life, and you do need His provision and blessing. God will bless you financially if He knows that you will pass it on. God wants to bring money to you and through you. He wants you to be a channel, not a reservoir.

SEED GIVING

Giving goes beyond the tenth. The tithing principle incorporates not only the person who receives a regular paycheck; it also includes the person who does not have regular monetary income, but does have material income that comes from herding, farming, growing, etc. Tithing is basically proportionate giving.

Giving goes beyond the tenth. Malachi 3:8 notes that we are not to rob God of "tithes and offerings." It is all a matter of achieving a proper balance. God does not expect you to give what you don't have.

In giving to God, we only return a portion of whatever He has already given us. The true spirit of giving brings on an automatic boomerang-like affect. Sowing, reaping, tithing and giving all overlap in some areas. Luke 6:38 tells us, "Give, and it shall be given unto you; good measure, pressed down, and shaken together, and running over, shall men give into your bosom. For with the same measure that ye mete withal it shall be measured to you again" (KJV).

Look at what this Scripture is really saying. It does in fact say that when we give, we will receive. This ties in closely with another verse found in Galatians 6:7, "Be not deceived; God is not mocked: for whatsoever a man soweth, that shall he also reap" (KJV). Giving is a seed and, if we sow it properly, God will see to it that we reap a harvest. According to Malachi 3:10, if we give properly of our tithes and offerings, God will open up the windows of heaven and pour out blessings that will be so great that we won't have room to receive them.

How much money should a Christian give to the Lord? Nowhere in the New Testament is this question answered. God is not so much interested in how much we give, whether it be the minimum of 10 percent, 15 percent, 20 percent, or even 50 percent of our income. He is interested in how and why we give. Second Corinthians 9:6–9 notes that the one who sows sparingly shall reap the same: "Remember this: Whoever sows sparingly will also reap sparingly, and whoever sows generously will also reap generously. Each man should give what he has decided in his heart to give, not reluctantly or under compulsion, for God loves a cheerful giver. And God is able to make all grace abound to you, so that in all things at all times, having all that you need, you will abound in every good work."

Second Corinthians 9:7 tells us how we should give. "Each man should give what he has decided in his heart to give, not reluctantly or under compulsion, for God loves a cheerful giver." We must be completely honest with ourselves. Do we honestly get a lot more enjoyment out of giving than we do out of receiving? Too many people put more emphasis on receiving than they do on giving. God's Word plainly teaches that all giving should be based upon love.

First Corinthians 13:3 tells this story; "If I give all I possess to the poor and surrender my body to the flames, but have not love, I gain nothing." Some people learn part of God's laws of prosperity and give in a calculating manner, anticipating something in return. This just isn't going to work. Giving without love is of no value whatsoever. No matter what we give, if our gift isn't based upon love, it is worth nothing. Love is the key to giving, and only love opens the channels for our loving Father to give back to us.
Systematic Giving

1 Corinthians 16:2–3

On the first day of every week, each one of you should set aside a sum of money in keeping with his income, saving it up, so that when I come no collections will have to be made.

A godly perspective on giving is found in this Scripture setting. In it Paul gives a direction and formula for consistent, regular giving. Note Paul's appeal for consistency. He asks for regular giving on the first day of the week. He asks specifically that a sum of money be set aside. Finally he asks for a proportionate amount that is in keeping with one's income.

Giving, like saving, needs to be regular, and it belongs in your budget for your place of worship. Your local church has regular financial challenges that must be met consistently.

17 GIVING COMMITMENTS

1. We Must Give to be Willing to Place All That We Have at God's Disposal.

Matthew 19:16–22

Now a man came up to Jesus and asked, "Teacher, what good thing must I do to get eternal life?" "Why do you ask me about what is good?" Jesus replied. "There is only One who is good. If you want to enter life, obey the commandments." "Which ones?" the man inquired. Jesus replied, "'Do not murder, do not commit adultery, do not steal, do not give false testimony, honor your father and mother,' and 'love your neighbor as yourself.'" "All these I have kept," the young man said. "What do I still lack?" Jesus answered, "If you want to be perfect, go, sell your possessions and give to the poor, and you will have treasure in heaven. Then come, follow me." When the young man heard this, he went away sad, because he had great wealth.

Wealth can keep us from inheriting the kingdom of heaven if it steals our heart from its rightful place in God's hands. In this story of the rich young man, Jesus could clearly see what was lord in his life. He was willing to obey Jesus until it came to money, obviously the true ruler of his heart. God does not ask each of us to sell our possessions and give to the poor, as He did this man, but the principle is still true today. It is about the willing heart. When we are truly surrendered to God's will in our lives, we have a heart that is willing to give everything to Him. When our hands are too busy grasping what God has given us, we are unable to receive more. Instead, we should live in such a way that we hold what God has given to us with open hands facing toward heaven. Such a posture says, "Whatever You've given me is Yours, Lord. I freely offer it." Notice, though, that when we offer, we are also in a position to receive.

Martin Luther once said: "People go through three conversions in the Christian faith: their head, their heart, and their pocketbook—unfortunately, not all at the same time!"

Exodus 35:5

> From what you have, take an offering for the LORD. Everyone who is willing is to bring to the LORD an offering of gold, silver and bronze...

We can see here that a willing heart is a must for giving offerings. God gave mankind a free will so that we would love Him freely. It is the same with offerings. He doesn't demand that we give above the tithe, but when we give out of our free will, we are telling Him that we love Him and it is our desire to worship Him with offerings.

2. We Must Give to Cultivate Our Faith.

Genesis 22:2–8

> Then God said, "Take your son, your only son, Isaac, whom you love, and go to the region of Moriah. Sacrifice him there as

a burnt offering on one of the mountains I will tell you about.'
Early the next morning Abraham got up and saddled his don-
key. He took with him two of his servants and his son Isaac.
When he had cut enough wood for the burnt offering, he set out
for the place God had told him about. On the third day Abra-
ham looked up and saw the place in the distance. He said to his
servants, 'Stay here with the donkey while I and the boy go over
there. We will worship and then we will come back to you."

Abraham took the wood for the burnt offering and placed it on
his son Isaac, and he himself carried the fire and the knife. As the
two of them went on together, Isaac spoke up and said to his father
Abraham, "Father?" "Yes, my son?" Abraham replied. "The fire
and wood are here," Isaac said, "but where is the lamb for the burnt
offering?" Abraham answered, "God himself will provide the lamb
for the burnt offering, my son." And the two of them went on together.

Genesis 22:11–13

But the angel of the LORD called out to him from heaven,
"Abraham! Abraham!" "Here I am," he replied. "Do not lay a
hand on the boy," He said. "Do not do anything to him. Now
I know that you fear God, because you have not withheld from
Me your son, your only son.'" Abraham looked up and there in
a thicket he saw a ram caught by its horns. He went over and
took the ram and sacrificed it as a burnt offering instead of his
son.

In this story, God asks Abraham to offer his only son, his be-
loved Isaac, on an altar as a sacrifice. Did God want Isaac to die?
No, verse 12 says that God's purpose was to see that Abraham truly
loved the Lord, and He did this by asking him to be willing to give
up his most prized "possession." Abraham passed the test and did
not withhold his son from God, but was willing to offer him.

One thing we might miss if we read the story too quickly is
the great faith of Abraham. Not only was Abraham willing to offer

his son, but he trusted the Lord with his offering. The Lord had promised Abraham that a great people would come from Isaac. Abraham's faith was to believe what God had promised even in the face of what could be the death of that promise. He did not hold too tightly, but instead when the Lord told him to offer a sacrifice, he was willing to obey. His faith meant knowing that, if the Lord had asked him to give an offering, He would also provide for the sacrifice (v. 8), one way or another.

Sometimes we are afraid to give too much because we want to be financially responsible. There is certainly a time for financial responsibility, but when God tells you to give an offering, it is time to trust Him! When God asks you to give something more than you think you can give, like Abraham you must have faith that God will provide the offering. A popular maxim today states, "God's will, His bill." When He speaks and we obey, He will provide. Let's give liberally and with great faith because we have a great God!

3. We Must Give to Bring Our Treasures.

Proverbs 15:6

> The house of the righteous contains great treasure, but the income of the wicked brings them trouble.

4. We Must Give to Express Our Worship.

2 Corinthians 8:7–8

> But just as you excel in everything—in faith, in speech, in knowledge, in complete earnestness and in your love for us— see that you also excel in this grace of giving. I am not commanding you, but I want to test the sincerity of your love by comparing it with the earnestness of others.

Giving an offering to God can be an expression of our worship. When we worship, we express our love to God. This is often done through singing and music, but 2 Corinthians 8:7 says that when we give above the tithe, it reflects the love in our heart and is in fact a test of the sincerity of our love.

Matthew 2:11

On coming to the house, they saw the child with his mother Mary, and they bowed down and worshiped him. Then they opened their treasures and presented him with gifts of gold and of incense and of myrrh.

When we follow the model of Jesus' first worshipers, the Magi who came from the east to worship Christ at His birth, we learn that giving is an important part of worship. These great men did two things in their worship of the newborn King. First, they bowed down. This is a symbol of surrender much like we do when we surrender our will for our lives and our finances to the will of the Father. Second, they gave their finest gifts. Let's worship God with our gifts and prove the sincerity of our love for Him.

5. We Must Give to Advance the Kingdom.

Matthew 6:19–21

"Do not store up for yourselves treasures on earth, where moth and rust destroy, and where thieves break in and steal. But store up for yourselves treasures in heaven, where moth and rust do not destroy, and where thieves do not break in and steal. For where your treasure is, there your heart will be also."

Throughout the centuries, mankind has been consumed with storing up earthly wealth—even to the investors of this present day, whose lives revolve around accumulating wealth for themselves and others. As Christians, we should be more concerned with investing into the kingdom of God, where our investments will reap eternal profit. How can we use our earthly treasure to increase the kingdom of heaven? This can be done by investing in our church, in people, and in land or buildings that will be used for the glory of God. Such things will bear fruit eternally as souls are saved and the harvest is reaped.

6. We Must Give Meet a Need

Matthew 25:34–40

"Then the King will say to those on his right, 'Come, you who are blessed by my Father; take your inheritance, the kingdom prepared for you since the creation of the world. For I was hungry and you gave me something to eat, I was thirsty and you gave me something to drink, I was a stranger and you invited me in, I needed clothes and you clothed me, I was sick and you looked after me, I was in prison and you came to visit me.' Then the righteous will answer him, 'Lord, when did we see you hungry and feed you, or thirsty and give you something to drink? When did we see you a stranger and invite you in, or needing clothes and clothe you? When did we see you sick or in prison and go to visit you?' "The King will reply, 'I tell you the truth, whatever you did for one of the least of these brothers of mine, you did for me.'"

As the body of Christ, we are accountable for the health and welfare of *all* parts of the body. We are also responsible for reflecting Christ's love to the needy. One of the most important ways to give to God is by meeting a need. Contact your local church to see if there are any needs you just might be able to meet.

Hebrews 13:16

And do not forget to do good and to share with others, for with such sacrifices God is pleased.

7. We Must Give With Liberality

Romans 12:4–8

For as we have many members in one body, but all the members do not have the same function, so we, being many, are one body in Christ, and individually members of one another. Having then gifts differing according to the grace that is given to us, let us use them: …he who gives, with liberality; he who leads, with diligence; he who shows mercy, with cheerfulness.

We all have our part to play in the body of Christ. Some of us have been given the gift of giving. We are encouraged not just to give, but to give with liberality. If God has called you to give, do so with a cheerfulness and liberality befitting one whose desire it is to add his or her part to the body of Christ.

8. We Must Give Out of Gratitude to God.

2 Corinthians 8:7–9

But just as you excel in everything—in faith, in speech, in knowledge, in complete earnestness and in your love for us—see that you also excel in this grace of giving. I am not commanding you, but I want to test the sincerity of your love by comparing it with the earnestness of others. For you know the grace of our Lord Jesus Christ, that though he was rich, yet for your sakes he became poor, so that you through his poverty might become rich.

The New Testament teaches that it is important for the believer to excel in the grace of giving. What is our motivation for this? We should be motivated by a desire to be like Christ. *For us,* Christ left heaven to become a man and die on the cross for our sins. He became spiritually poor for a lifetime, as it were, that we may be rich for eternity. Though God does not ask us to be poor, we should be motivated out of our heart of love and gratefulness to give as He did. Let us be like Christ and give, reflecting His love to those around us.

9. We Must Give Because God is the Owner; We are the Stewards.

1 Corinthians 4:1–2

> Let a man so consider us, as servants of Christ and stewards of the mysteries of God. Moreover it is required in stewards that one be found faithful.

Luke 16:13

> "No servant can serve two masters. Either he will hate the one and love the other, or he will be devoted to the one and despise the other. You cannot serve both God and Money."

This verse in Luke makes it clear that we will either serve God or money and that it is impossible to serve both. We must take our positions as stewards of money seriously and carefully guard God's interests, not our own. We should protect and increase His property with the money we are entrusted with.

10. We Must Give Because God Commissions us to Provide for His Servants.

Ezra 1:2–4

> This is what Cyrus king of Persia says: "The LORD, the God of heaven, has given me all the kingdoms of the earth and he has appointed me to build a temple for him at Jerusalem in Judah. Anyone of his people among you — may his God be with him, and let him go up to Jerusalem in Judah and build the temple of the LORD, the God of Israel, the God who is in Jerusalem. And the people of any place where survivors may now be living are to provide him with silver and gold, with goods and livestock, and with freewill offerings for the temple of God in Jerusalem."

In this passage, Ezra recounts a very special season in the history of God's people. The people of God were being commissioned to build His temple in Jerusalem, and the king would allow any of the Israelites who wanted to build it to go. Who was going to support these servants who were willing to leave their homes and families in order to build God's temple? The Israelites from that servant's hometown were to provide him with silver and gold, with goods and livestock. How wonderful it is to see throughout this book how the neighbors of these servants of God provided for the building of the temple in Jerusalem. All the Israelites living in Persia were expected to give freewill offerings for God's temple in Jerusalem, and they rose to the occasion, seeing God's house built and God glorified.

We may not all be Israelites, but we are God's people. We may not be building a temple for God in Jerusalem, but we should be building His house throughout the world. "But you will receive power when the Holy Spirit comes on you; and you will be my witnesses in Jerusalem, and in all Judea and Samaria, and to the ends of the earth" (Acts 1:8).

For those who do go, leaving homes and families for a season in order to fulfill the great commission, who is to provide? According to this biblical model, those who stay should provide for God's servants with finances, goods, food, etc. This sure sounds like a Great Commission to me!

In addition, we should consider giving freewill offerings for the building of God's house throughout the world, just as the Israelites were commissioned to in Ezra's day. These offerings were given in the local congregation and consecrated to the Lord for the building of His house elsewhere (Ezra 3:5). These offerings were designated "freewill" offerings, given out of the liberality of one's heart. God does not require us to give more than 10 percent, but it sure is wonderful when we rise to the occasion and see God's house built. Let's allow God to speak to us about missions and supporting His work worldwide.

11. We Must Give so God is glorified.

Psalm 96:8

Give to the LORD the glory due His name; bring an offering, and come into His courts.

The psalms, a favorite portion of Scripture for many believers, often describe the glory of God as well as ways we can glorify Him. One such way, as revealed by Psalm 96:8, is by bringing an offering. It brings glory to God when we come into His presence with an offering. We often think of coming into His presence with thanksgiving (Psalm 95:2) and with singing (Psalm 100:2), but this verse says we can come into His presence with an offering. Bringing an offering is an act of thanksgiving for what He's given us, and it is an act of praise. Let's glorify the Lord, as we give offerings with a heart of thankfulness.

12. We Must Give Because We Love the House of God

1 Chronicles 29:3

Moreover, because I have set my affection on the house of my God, I have given to the house of my God, over and above all that I have prepared for the holy house, my own special treasure of gold and silver…

We should love the house of God. We should love His presence, and we should love His people. As believers, we should cultivate a love for the house of God, just as the worshiper David did. This great affection for God and all that is His should motivate us to give because we want to see His house prosper in great splendor. While contemporary churches are not often built with gold and silver, we can invest in people and in His work, putting action to our love for the house of God.

13. We Must Give Because God is Faithful.

Proverbs 19:17

> *He who has pity on the poor lends to the LORD, and He will pay back what he has given.*

God is so faithful when we step out in obedience to Him. It is important for us to care for the needy around us and trust God to meet our needs. The generous can look to the wealth of promises in God's Word and know that He will be faithful to supply every need.

14. We Must Give Because It's in Our New Nature.

Romans 7:14–23

> *We know that the law is spiritual; but I am unspiritual, sold as a slave to sin. I do not understand what I do. For what I want to do I do not do, but what I hate I do. And if I do what I do not want to do, I agree that the law is good. As it is, it is no longer I myself who do it, but it is sin living in me. I know that nothing good lives in me, that is, in my sinful nature. For I have the desire to do what is good, but I cannot carry it out. For what I do is not the good I want to do; no, the evil I do not want to do — this I keep on doing. Now if I do what I do not want to do, it is no longer I who do it, but it is sin living in me that does it.*
>
> *So I find this law at work: When I want to do good, evil is right there with me. For in my inner being I delight in God's law; but I see another law at work in the members of my body, waging war against the law of my mind and making me a prisoner of the law of sin at work within my members.*

When we refer to our "old nature," we refer to everything that we inherited from Adam. It reflects everything in our life that falls outside the newness we have in Christ. The old nature is stubborn, delights in sin, and condones sin. Romans 7 talks about the conflict between our old nature, which is sensual, carnal, and unspiritual, made of weak flesh, sold to the slavery of sin. When we live according to the flesh, there is confusion within the spirit that has been redeemed by God. When we live according to our old nature, we are working against the will of our own spirit. Sometimes as Christians, we even do exactly the things we should hate.

Sin drives the old nature. Though our spirit may be willing to do what is right, the flesh seems too weak to carry it out. We in ourselves do not have the strength to do what is right. Precisely when we begin to desire the right things, sin seems to attack! This battle can be wearisome.

2 Corinthians 5:17

Therefore, if anyone is in Christ, he is a new creation; the old has gone, the new has come!

Romans 1:17

For in the gospel a righteousness from God is revealed, a righteousness that is by faith from first to last, just as it is written: "The righteous will live by faith."

2 Corinthians 4:16

Therefore we do not lose heart. Though outwardly we are wasting away, yet inwardly we are being renewed day by day.

Christ provides us with a new nature and the strength to follow through. Faith is to live in His strength, not relying on our own strength to do what is right. Not only does God make us righteous, but He renews us inwardly. As believers, we need to live according to the new nature. As Colossians says, we must "put on the new self," daily living as Christ would want us to. As we allow our minds and spirits to be renewed, we will live in a way that reflects His generous nature.

Colossians 3:10

And have put on the new self, which is being renewed in knowledge in the image of its Creator.

15. We Must Give to Develop an Eternal Perspective

Our perspective is the way that we look at situations or topics. Perspective determines our ability to evaluate properly the relative importance of things. The word perspective used to mean a telescope or glass through which items were viewed. It is our viewpoint, outlook, point of view, or the way that we perceive things. God's people are to have an eternal perspective.

1 Timothy 6:17–19

Command those who are rich in this present world not to be arrogant nor to put their hope in wealth, which is so uncertain, but to put their hope in God, who richly provides us with everything for our enjoyment. Command them to do good, to be rich in good deeds, and to be generous and willing to share. In this way they will lay up treasure for themselves as a firm foundation for the coming age, so that they may take hold of the life that is truly life.

The Lord desires that we see wealth with an eternal perspective. We are not to put our hope in wealth that comes and goes, but we are to trust Him who provides. We are to use our wealth for good, always ready to give in generosity. Giving is to invest in treasure that will not fade, eternal treasure. When we give our wealth instead of using it for earthly pleasures, we reflect that we are citizens of heaven and are keeping an eternal perspective.

Matthew 6:28–33

"And why do you worry about clothes? See how the lilies of the field grow. They do not labor or spin. Yet I tell you that not even Solomon in all his splendor was dressed like one of these. If that

is how God clothes the grass of the field, which is here today and tomorrow is thrown into the fire, will he not much more clothe you, O you of little faith? So do not worry, saying, 'What shall we eat?' or 'What shall we drink?' or 'What shall we wear?' For the pagans run after all these things, and your heavenly Father knows that you need them. But seek first his kingdom and his righteousness, and all these things will be given to you as well."

Out of our trust in God, we can seek the good of God's kingdom first, knowing that God will take care of our own needs.

Luke 12:33

Sell your possessions and give to the poor. Provide purses for yourselves that will not wear out, a treasure in heaven that will not be exhausted, where no thief comes near and no moth destroys.

16. We Must Give Because God is Good.

Matthew 12:35

"The good man brings good things out of the good stored up in him, and the evil man brings evil things out of the evil stored up in him."

When our hearts are filled with the goodness of God, we will give out of that goodness. Let's allow our hearts to be filled with these truths about God's goodness.

- God is gracious and compassionate. (Exodus 33:19; 34:6)

- God wants to bless you. (Psalm 21:3)

- God wants to allow His goodness to be with you always. (Psalm 23:6)

- God prepares good things for those who fear Him. (Psalm 31:19)

- God gives the power to get wealth. (Deuteronomy 8:18)

- God gives strength and power to His people. (Psalm 68:35)

- God gives life to the world. (John 6:33)

- God gives us richly all things to enjoy. (1 Timothy 6:17)

- God has the power to do anything. (Isaiah 40:21–22)

- God has the power to create something from nothing. (Psalm 33:6–9)

- God is sovereign and there is nothing too hard for Him. (Jeremiah 32:17–19)

17. We Must Give to Discover God's Response.

Proverbs 3:9–10

> *Honor the LORD with your wealth, with the firstfruits of all your crops; then your barns will be filled to overflowing, and your vats will brim over with new wine.*

When we give, we activate the supernatural law of God, releasing Him to work in our private lives. God responds when we honor Him with our wealth by opening opportunities to receive divine provision both directly and indirectly. His desire is to bless us abundantly so that we might have more than enough, releasing us, in turn, to give even more liberally.

Proverbs 22:9

> *He who has a generous eye will be blessed, for he gives of his bread to the poor.*

2 Corinthians 9:7–8

> *So let each one give as he purposes in his heart, not grudgingly or of necessity; for God loves a cheerful giver. And God is able to make all grace abound toward you, that you, always having*

all sufficiency in all things, may have an abundance for every good work.

Proverbs 11:24–26

There is one who scatters, yet increases more; and there is one who withholds more than is right, but it leads to poverty. The generous soul will be made rich, and he who waters will also be watered himself. The people will curse him who withholds grain, but blessing will be on the head of him who sells it.

Generosity is the key characteristic of the blessed, because God blesses those who have a generous heart. Not only will He bless us so that we feel blessed, but He also provides for us so that we can bless others! When we give, God makes all grace abound toward us so that we will always have a sufficient amount for all our needs—and an abundance to be able to give to every good work. Does this sound like a bounty of blessing or what!

Proverbs 10:22

The blessing of the Lord brings wealth, and he adds no trouble to it.

CHAPTER 6

Your Giving Questions...Answered

WHAT SHOULD MY GIVING ATTITUDE BE?

Luke 21:1–3

> *As he looked up, Jesus saw the rich putting their gifts into the temple treasury. He also saw a poor widow put in two very small copper coins. "I tell you the truth," he said, "this poor widow has put in more than all the others.*
>
> *"All these people gave their gifts out of their wealth; but she out of her poverty put in all she had to live on."*

The widow was poor, perhaps destitute. She has a couple of coins to pay for her next meal or two, but that's it. Her desire to give to God was so powerful that she pulled both coins from her pocket and gave all she had.

She gave cheerfully to the work of the kingdom. No one saw her do it. No one knew what she gave. No one understood that she gave it all. No one even noticed...no one, except Jesus. Jesus knew the depth of her sacrifice. Jesus knew what it cost her. All of the other givers on that day gave out of their abundance, out of their wealth. She gave out of her poverty.

This woman is a model for us in giving with the right motivation. When Jesus spoke about giving in His Sermon on the Mount, He taught that the motivation for giving should not be to receive the praise of men or to impress men with our wealth or generosity. Instead, we should be so focused on pleasing God that we do not even allow men to see that we are giving.

Matthew 6:1- 4

"Take heed that you do not do your charitable deeds before men, to be seen by them. Otherwise you have no reward from your Father in heaven. Therefore, when you do a charitable deed, do not sound a trumpet before you as the hypocrites do in the synagogues and in the streets, that they may have glory from men. Assuredly, I say to you, they have their reward. But when you do a charitable deed, do not let your left hand know what your right hand is doing, that your charitable deed may be in secret; and your Father who sees in secret will Himself reward you openly."

WHAT IS PROPORTIONAL GIVING?

Luke 12:48

"From everyone who has been given much, much will be demanded; and from the one who has been entrusted with much, much more will be asked."

1 Corinthians 16:2

On the first day of every week, each one of you should set aside a sum of money in keeping with his income, saving it up, so that when I come no collections will have to be made.

WHAT IS SACRIFICIAL GIVING?

2 Corinthians 8:1–4

And now, brothers, we want you to know about the grace that God has given the Macedonian churches. Out of the most severe trial, their overflowing joy and their extreme poverty welled up in rich generosity. For I testify that they gave as much as they were able, and even beyond their ability. Entirely on their own, they urgently pleaded with us for the privilege of sharing in this service to the saints.

The Macedonian churches are commended as models to the churches of Corinth in the grace of giving. One could assume that the Macedonians must have been rich to be able to give so much and yet this passage teaches otherwise. Paul wrote that their rich generosity came out of extreme poverty! You probably can't say that you are living in extreme poverty, and yet these extremely poor people were called richly generous. They gave not only what they were able, but, "even beyond their ability."

We know from history that these churches had been hit by an earthquake. This natural catastrophe had destroyed cities and ruined the economy. These churches were experiencing great tribulation, but the grace of God was there. He put generosity in the hearts of these churches and enabled them to give, in spite of their desperate circumstances. The Expositor's Bible says this of the Macedonians: "They gave far more generously than their slender means and adverse circumstances really permitted them. Not that their judgment was imbalanced, but their eagerness to contribute led them to surpass all expectations!" True givers give sacrificially, not just out of their surplus.

What was the heart of the Macedonian churches when giving more than they felt they could? Second Corinthians 8:2 says that they gave with overflowing joy, even out of the most severe trial. They counted it a privilege to share in the service of giving to the saints. What a tremendous example these churches can be to us in sacrificial giving. As we give liberally and with joy in our hearts, even in the face of our own lack, God supplies and makes more giving possible.

Matthew 6:4

"...so that your giving may be in secret. Then your Father, who sees what is done in secret, will reward you."

When it comes to the giving commitment of some senior citizens on a small fixed income, many would want to tell them to keep the money for their own use. But in the story of the widow who gave all and gave out of her poverty, Christ let her do it.

He didn't stop her, knowing what a tremendous sacrifice she was making. Did God need her two coins? Of course not. It was barely enough to buy a single meal for the poor—and she qualified for that meal herself. Others may not know of your sacrificial giving, but God knows.

2 Samuel 24:24

But the king replied to Araunah, "No, I insist on paying you for it. I will not sacrifice to the LORD my God burnt offerings that cost me nothing." So David bought the threshing floor and the oxen and paid fifty shekels of silver for them.

Even King David, one of the richest men of biblical times, understood the principle of sacrificial giving. He would not give an offering that cost him nothing. It can sometimes be so easy to give something that costs us nothing or that we wouldn't mind getting rid of, but God sees the heart. If we do not value our offering, why should He? He craves our willingness to sacrifice out of pure love for Him.

What Is Faithful Giving?

Deuteronomy 23:21

If you make a vow to the LORD your God, do not be slow to pay it, for the LORD your God will certainly demand it of you and you will be guilty of sin.

2 Corinthians 8:10–11

And here is my advice about what is best for you in this matter: Last year you were the first not only to give but also to have the desire to do so. Now finish the work, so that your eager willingness to do it may be matched by your completion of it, according to your means.

We as Christians should all have the earnest desire to give as our nature is transformed to reflect the character of Christ. However, that eager willingness is not the end point, but the beginning point that motivates us toward action. The Corinthian church in the New Testament had committed to give an offering, and their heart was behind it. In this passage, however, they had not yet given to the full extent of their commitment. Paul emphasizes in his second letter to them the importance of being faithful to follow through and give what they had committed to.

So often, our heart is right and we have the best intentions. Unfortunately, with our human nature still vying for control, we can easily push our giving commitments to the back of our minds or reason our way out of giving to the full extent of our original intentions. The fact of the matter is that good intentions don't produce results if there is no accompanying action. Let's be faithful in our giving commitments, for God rewards faithfulness.

Proverbs 28:20

A faithful man will be richly blessed, but one eager to get rich will not go unpunished.

What Is Faith Giving?

When Malachi refers to bringing all of the tithes into the storehouse, he challenges us to test or prove that our tithes unleash the blessing of God. We often refer to it as "open heavens." "Prove me, test me, etc.," is an operation of faith. It is a principle of giving that we are challenged to put into practice.

Genesis 8:22

As long as the earth endures, seedtime and harvest, cold and heat, summer and winter, day and night will never cease.

True givers give in faith, recognizing the laws of harvest. An offering given in faith is like a seed given by the believer and sowed in faith, trusting God to water it and enable it to become the full harvest of what God desires to bring in that believer's life.

Psalm 126:6

He who goes out weeping, carrying seed to sow, will return with songs of joy, carrying sheaves with him.

As this psalm expresses, it can sometimes be a challenge to sow our own personal resources into the field of God's will. It is difficult to trust God, but when we do, we will reap returns. These returns may be financial, but, then again, they may not be. God's desire is to bless us, but money is not the end goal. The way He blesses us may simply be by giving us joy in seeing our resources used to advance God's kingdom. One thing we can know for sure is that we will be blessed, and God will provide for all of our needs.

2 Corinthians 9:6–11

Remember this: Whoever sows sparingly will also reap sparingly, and whoever sows generously will also reap generously. Each man should give what he has decided in his heart to give, not reluctantly or under compulsion, for God loves a cheerful giver. And God is able to make all grace abound to you, so that

in all things at all times, having all that you need, you will
abound in every good work. As it is written: "He has scattered
abroad his gifts to the poor; his righteousness endures forever."
Now he who supplies seed to the sower and bread for food will
also supply and increase your store of seed and will enlarge the
harvest of your righteousness. You will be made rich in every
way so that you can be generous on every occasion, and through
us your generosity will result in thanksgiving to God.

He who supplies will supply and increase and enlarge the harvest for these true givers. According to the promises of God in these verses, the generous giver will be made rich in every way so that he can be generous on every occasion. Psalm 18:30 says, "As for God, His way is perfect; the word of the LORD is proven; he is a shield to all who trust in Him" (NKJV). When we truly believe God's promises, we can be free to give what is in our heart, having faith that God will be faithful to His word.

Galatians 6:9

Let us not become weary in doing good, for at the proper time
we will reap a harvest if we do not give up.

What Is Obedient Giving?

Deuteronomy 28:2

All these blessings will come upon you and accompany you if
you obey the LORD your God.

Job 36:11

If they obey and serve him, they will spend the rest of their days
in prosperity and their years in contentment.

There are many blessing promises in the Bible, but it takes an act of obedience on our part to activate God's blessings. When we are obedient, it triggers His blessing reaction process. God is more willing to fulfill His promises than we are to receive them. He is always faithful.

As in the story of the widow of Zarephath in 1 Kings 17:8–16, when God speaks and we obey, our giving can release supernatural provision in our lives, as well as the lives of others. This woman had no hope, no future, and no provision when the prophet came and told her to give up her last meal. No one could discredit her if she chose not to, saving her son for one more day. Instead of trusting in the natural, she learned to trust in the Lord. She experienced supernatural provision as a result of trusting in His word.

Exodus 35:21

> Then everyone came whose heart was stirred, and everyone whose spirit was willing, and they brought the Lord's offering for the work of the tabernacle of meeting, for all its service, and for the holy garments.

When God stirs our heart to give, it is important that we heed the voice of the Holy Spirit and obey. Jesus said that if we love Him, we will obey Him: "Blessed rather are those who hear the word of God and obey it" (Luke 11:28).

What Is Worship Giving?

Genesis 4:3–4

> In the course of time Cain brought some of the fruits of the soil as an offering to the LORD. But Abel brought fat portions from some of the firstborn of his flock. The LORD looked with favor on Abel and his offering.

Cain and Abel gave to God as an act of worship.

WHAT IS GRATEFUL GIVING?

Remember the goodness of God. What has God given to you? Here are a few possibilities: family, children, employment, church, friends, health, etc. When you give with a grateful heart, you are not asking the question "do I have to give?" rather you are rejoicing that "you can give."

Psalm 37:4

Delight yourself in the LORD and he will give you the desires of your heart.

Psalm 107:22

Let them sacrifice thank offerings and tell of his works with songs of joy.

Psalm 100:4

Enter his gates with thanksgiving and his courts with praise; give thanks to him and praise his name.

Matthew 10:8

"Freely you have received, freely give."

WHAT IS INVESTMENT GIVING?

Luke 12:32–34

"Sell your possessions and give to the poor. Provide purses for yourselves that will not wear out, a treasure in heaven that will not be exhausted, where no thief comes near and no moth destroys. For where your treasure is, there your heart will be also."

1 Timothy 6:18–19

Command them to do good, to be rich in good deeds, and to be generous and willing to share. In this way they will lay up treasure for themselves as a firm foundation for the coming age, so that they may take hold of the life that is truly life.

Psalm 37:16

Better the little that the righteous have than the wealth of many wicked.

CHAPTER 7

How We Are To Give

WE MUST GIVE OUR FIRSTFRUITS

Exodus 23:19a

The first of the firstfruits of your land you shall bring into the house of the LORD your God. (NKJV)

Deuteronomy 18:4

The firstfruits of your grain and your new wine and your oil, and the first of the fleece of your sheep, you shall give him. (NKJV)

Numbers 18:29–30, 32

Of all your gifts you shall offer up every heave offering due to the LORD, from all the best of them, the consecrated part of them. Therefore you shall say to them: "When you have lifted up the best of it, then the rest shall be accounted to the Levites as the produce of the threshing floor and as the produce of the winepress. And you shall bear no sin because of it, when you have lifted up the best of it. But you shall not profane the holy gifts of the children of Israel, lest you die.: (NKJV)

Proverbs 3:9

Honor the LORD with your possessions, and with the first-fruits of all your increase. (NKJV)

Ezekiel 20:40

"For on My holy mountain, on the mountain height of Israel," says the Lord GOD, "there all the house of Israel, all of them in the land, shall serve Me; there I will accept them, and there I will require your offerings and the firstfruits of your sacrifices, together with all your holy things." (NKJV)

Ezekiel 44:30

There were archways all around, twenty-five cubits long and five cubits wide. (NKJV)

WE MUST GIVE ACCORDING TO OUR BLESSING

Mark 12:41–44

The Widow's Two Mites (Luke 21:1–4): Now Jesus sat opposite the treasury and saw how the people put money into the treasury. And many who were rich put in much. Then one poor widow came and threw in two mites, which make a quadrans. So He called His disciples to Himself and said to them, "Assuredly, I say to you that this poor widow has put in more than all those who have given to the treasury; for they all put in out of their abundance, but she out of her poverty put in all that she had, her whole livelihood." (NKJV)

11:29

Then the disciples, each according to his ability, determined to send relief to the brethren dwelling in Judea. (NKJV.)

1 Corinthians 16:2

On the first day of the week let each one of you lay something aside, storing up as he may prosper, that there be no collections when I come. (NKJV)

2 Corinthians 8:12–14

For if there is first a willing mind, it is accepted according to what one has, and not according to what he does not have. For I do not mean that others should be eased and you burdened; but by an equality, that now at this time your abundance may supply their lack, that their abundance also may supply your lack—that there may be equality. (NKJV)

WE MUST GIVE OUT OF GRATITUDE

Deuteronomy 26:9–10

He has brought us to this place and has given us this land, "a land flowing with milk and honey"; and now, behold, I have brought the firstfruits of the land which you, O LORD, have given me. "Then you shall set it before the LORD your God, and worship before the LORD your God." (NKJV)

1 Chronicles 29:14

But who am I, and who are my people, that we should be able to offer so willingly as this? For all things come from You, and of Your own we have given You. (NKJV)

Matthew 10:8

"Heal the sick, cleanse the lepers, raise the dead, cast out demons. Freely you have received, freely give." (NKJV)

Ephesians 5:1–2

Walk in Love. Therefore be imitators of God as dear children. And walk in love, as Christ also has loved us and given Himself for us, an offering and a sacrifice to God for a sweet-smelling aroma. (NKJV)

We Must Give To Assist the Needy

Deuteronomy 15:7–11

Generosity to the Poor

If there is among you a poor man of your brethren, within any of the gates in your land which the LORD your God is giving you, you shall not harden your heart nor shut your hand from your poor brother, but you shall open your hand wide to him and willingly lend him sufficient for his need, whatever he needs. Beware lest there be a wicked thought in your heart, saying, "The seventh year, the year of release, is at hand," and your eye be evil against your poor brother and you give him nothing, and he cry out to the LORD against you, and it become sin among you. You shall surely give to him, and your heart should not be grieved when you give to him, because for this thing the LORD your God will bless you in all your works and in all to which you put your hand. For the poor will never cease from the land; therefore I command you, saying, "You shall open your hand wide to your brother, to your poor and your needy, in your land." (NKJV)

Deuteronomy 26:12

When you have finished laying aside all the tithe of your increase in the third year—the year of tithing—and have given it to the Levite, the stranger, the fatherless, and the widow, so that they may eat within your gates and be filled. (NKJV)

Proverbs 28:27

He who gives to the poor will not lack, But he who hides his eyes will have many curses. (NKJV)

Isaiah 58:6–9

Is this not the fast that I have chosen: to loose the bonds of wickedness, to undo the heavy burdens, to let the oppressed go free, And that you break every yoke? Is it not to share your bread with the hungry, And that you bring to your house the poor who are cast out; When you see the naked, that you cover him, And not hide yourself from your own flesh? Then your light shall break forth like the morning, Your healing shall spring forth speedily, And your righteousness shall go before you; The glory of the LORD shall be your rear guard. Then you shall call, and the LORD will answer; you shall cry, and He will say, "Here I am." If you take away the yoke from your midst, The pointing of the finger, and speaking wickedness. (NKJV)

Matthew 19:21

Jesus said to him, "If you want to be perfect, go, sell what you have and give to the poor, and you will have treasure in heaven; and come, follow Me." (NKJV)

Luke 10:33–35

"But a certain Samaritan, as he journeyed, came where he was. And when he saw him, he had compassion. So he went to him and bandaged his wounds, pouring on oil and wine; and he set

him on his own animal, brought him to an inn, and took care of him. On the next day, when he departed, he took out two denarii, gave them to the innkeeper, and said to him, 'Take care of him; and whatever more you spend, when I come again, I will repay you.'" (NKJV)

Luke 12:33

"Sell what you have and give alms; provide yourselves money bags which do not grow old, a treasure in the heavens that does not fail, where no thief approaches nor moth destroys." (NKJV)

Sharing in All Things

Acts 4:32–35

Now the multitude of those who believed were of one heart and one soul; neither did anyone say that any of the things he possessed was his own, but they had all things in common. And with great power the apostles gave witness to the resurrection of the Lord Jesus. And great grace was upon them all. Nor was there anyone among them who lacked; for all who were possessors of lands or houses sold them, and brought the proceeds of the things that were sold, and laid them at the apostles' feet; and they distributed to each as anyone had need. (NKJV)

WE MUST GIVE AS JESUS GAVE

Every time we see a picture of Christ in the Bible, He is giving. He always *gave*, and it always cost Him something.

- Jesus *gave* new wine to two lovers who started down the road of "till death do us part" (John 2:1–11).

- Jesus *gave* living water to a woman of Samaria who apparently came to Jacob's well at the sixth hour to avoid the stares of those who disapproved of her marriage (John

4:1–42).

- Jesus *gave* a miracle of healing to a cripple at the pool by the sheep market who had waited thirty-eight years to walk and run and jump (John 5:1–9).

- Jesus *gave* a son back to the widow of Nain as she was tearfully and lovingly taking his remains to the cemetery (Luke 7:11–15).

- Jesus *gave* the light of the day to a man who all of his life had lived in the darkness of the world of the blind (John 9).

- Jesus *gave* forgiveness to a woman caught in the very act of adultery (John 8:3–11).

- Jesus *gave* Lazarus back to Mary and Martha! FIVE important words were spoken at the grave: "Take ye away the stone."

- Jesus *gave* bread. In Luke 22:19 Jesus "took bread, and gave thanks, and brake it, and gave unto them, saying, This is my body which is given for you: this do in remembrance of me."

- Jesus *gave* His head to be crowned with thorns. He gave His back to be slashed by the cat-o'-nine-tails.

- He *gave* His feet to the lonely Calvary road. He gave His shoulders to the overwhelming weight of the cross.

- Our Lord *gave* His loving, tender hands to the cruel spikes and He gave His body to the cross.

- Jesus *gave* His life. In John 10:11, Jesus said, "I am the good shepherd: the good shepherd giveth his life for the sheep."

- He *gave* His Spirit to the Father and gave His body to the borrowed tomb.

- According to Titus 2:14, Jesus "*gave* himself for us, that he might redeem us from all iniquity, and purify unto himself a peculiar people, zealous of good works."

- God *gave* His Son: "For God so loved the world, that he gave his only begotten Son, that *whosoever* believeth in him should not perish, but have everlasting life" (John 3:16).

WE MUST GIVE AS ABRAHAM (ABRAM) GAVE

Genesis 14:18–20

Then Melchizedek king of Salem brought out bread and wine; he was the priest of God Most High. And he blessed him and said: "Blessed be Abram of God Most High, possessor of heaven and earth; and blessed be God Most High, Who has delivered your enemies into your hand." And he gave him a tithe of all. (NKJV)

WE MUST GIVE AS BOAZ, HUSBAND OF RUTH, GAVE

Ruth 2:5–9

Then Boaz said to his servant who was in charge of the reapers, "Whose young woman is this?" So the servant who was in charge of the reapers answered and said, "It is the young Moabite woman who came back with Naomi from the country of Moab. And she said, 'Please let me glean and gather after the reapers among the sheaves.' So she came and has continued from morning until now, though she rested a little in the house." Then Boaz said to Ruth, "You will listen, my daughter, will you not? Do not go to glean in another field, nor go from here, but stay close by my young women. Let your eyes be on the field which they reap, and go after them. Have I not commanded the young men not to touch you? And when you are thirsty, go to the vessels and drink from what the young men have drawn." (NKJV)

WE MUST GIVE AS CORNELIUS, THE ROMAN SOLDIER, GAVE

Acts 10:1–2

> *There was a certain man in Caesarea called Cornelius, a centurion of what was called the Italian Regiment, a devout man and one who feared God with all his household, who gave alms generously to the people, and prayed to God always. (NKJV)*

WE MUST GIVE AS DAVID, THE KING, GAVE

2 Samuel 24:18–25

> *And Gad came that day to David and said to him, "Go up, erect an altar to the LORD on the threshing floor of Araunah the Jebusite." So David, according to the word of Gad, went up as the LORD commanded. Now Araunah looked, and saw the king and his servants coming toward him. So Araunah went out and bowed before the king with his face to the ground. Then Araunah said, "Why has my lord the king come to his servant?" And David said, "To buy the threshing floor from you, to build an altar to the LORD, that the plague may be withdrawn from the people." Now Araunah said to David, "Let my lord the king take and offer up whatever seems good to him. Look, here are oxen for burnt sacrifice, and threshing implements and the yokes of the oxen for wood. All these, O king, Araunah has given to the king." And Araunah said to the king, "May the LORD your God accept you." Then the king said to Araunah, "No, but I will surely buy it from you for a price; nor will I offer burnt offerings to the LORD my God with that which costs me nothing." So David bought the threshing floor and the oxen for fifty shekels of silver. And David built there an altar to the LORD, and offered burnt offerings and peace offerings. So the LORD heeded the prayers for the land, and the plague was withdrawn from Israel. (NKJV)*

WE MUST GIVE AS JACOB, SON OF ISAAC AND REBEKAH, GRANDSON OF ABRAHAM, GAVE

Genesis 28:20–22

Then Jacob made a vow, saying, "If God will be with me, and keep me in this way that I am going, and give me bread to eat and clothing to put on, so that I come back to my father's house in peace, then the LORD shall be my God. And this stone which I have set as a pillar shall be God's house, and of all that You give me I will surely give a tenth to You." (NKJV)

WE MUST GIVE AS KING HEZEKIAH, THIRTEENTH KING OF JUDAH, GAVE

2 Chronicles 31:3

The king also appointed a portion of his possessions for the burnt offerings: for the morning and evening burnt offerings, the burnt offerings for the Sabbaths and the New Moons and the set feasts, as it is written in the Law of the LORD. (NKJV)

WE MUST GIVE AS THE LORD JESUS CHRIST GAVE

Mark 10:45

"For even the Son of Man did not come to be served, but to serve, and to give His life a ransom for many." (NKJV)

John 3:16

"For God so loved the world that He gave His only begotten Son, that whoever believes in Him should not perish but have everlasting life." (NKJV)

2 Corinthians 8:9

For you know the grace of our Lord Jesus Christ, that though He was rich, yet for your sakes He became poor, that you through His poverty might become rich. (NKJV)

Luke 8:1–3

Now it came to pass, afterward, that He went through every city and village, preaching and bringing the glad tidings of the kingdom of God. And the twelve were with Him, and certain women who had been healed of evil spirits and infirmities— Mary called Magdalene, out of whom had come seven demons, and Joanna the wife of Chuza, Herod's steward, and Susanna, and many others who provided for Him from their substance. (NKJV)

Matthew 22:15–22

Then the Pharisees went and plotted how they might entangle Him in His talk. And they sent to Him their disciples with the Herodians, saying, "Teacher, we know that You are true, and teach the way of God in truth; nor do You care about anyone, for You do not regard the person of men. Tell us, therefore, what do You think? Is it lawful to pay taxes to Caesar, or not?" But Jesus perceived their wickedness, and said, "Why do you test Me, you hypocrites? Show Me the tax money." So they brought Him a denarius. And He said to them, "Whose image and inscription is this?" They said to Him, "Caesar's." And He said to them, "Render therefore to Caesar the things that are Caesar's, and to God the things that are God's." When they had heard these words, they marveled, and left Him and went their way. (NKJV)

Mark 12:13–17

Then they sent to Him some of the Pharisees and the Herodians, to catch Him in His words. When they had come, they said to Him, "Teacher, we know that You are true, and care about no one; for You do not regard the person of men, but teach the way of God in truth. Is it lawful to pay taxes to Caesar, or not? Shall we pay, or shall we not pay?" But He, knowing their hypocrisy, said to them, "Why do you test Me? Bring Me a denarius that I may see it." So they brought it. And He said to them, "Whose image and inscription is this?" And they said to Him, "Caesar's." And Jesus answered and said to them, "Render to Caesar the things that are Caesar's, and to God the things that are God's." And they marveled at Him. (NKJV)

Luke 20:20–26

So they watched Him, and sent spies who pretended to be righteous, that they might seize on His words, in order to deliver Him to the power and the authority of the governor. Then they asked Him, saying, "Teacher, we know that You say and teach rightly, and You do not show personal favoritism, but teach the way of God in truth: Is it lawful for us to pay taxes to Caesar or not?" But He perceived their craftiness, and said to them, "Why do you test Me? Show Me a denarius. Whose image and inscription does it have?" They answered and said, "Caesar's." And He said to them, "Render therefore to Caesar the things that are Caesar's, and to God the things that are God's." But they could not catch Him in His words in the presence of the people. And they marveled at His answer and kept silent. (NKJV)

WE MUST GIVE AS
THE CHRISTIANS FROM PHILIPPI GAVE

Philippians 4:15–18

Now you Philippians know also that in the beginning of the gospel, when I departed from Macedonia, no church shared with me concerning giving and receiving but you only. For even in Thessalonica you sent aid once and again for my necessities. Not that I seek the gift, but I seek the fruit that abounds to your account. Indeed I have all and abound. I am full, having received from Epaphroditus the things sent from you, a sweet-smelling aroma, an acceptable sacrifice, well pleasing to God. (NKJV)

WE MUST GIVE AS THE CHRISTIANS OF THE
MACEDONIAN CHURCHES GAVE

2 Corinthians 8:1–6

Moreover, brethren, we make known to you the grace of God bestowed on the churches of Macedonia: that in a great trial of affliction the abundance of their joy and their deep poverty abounded in the riches of their liberality. For I bear witness that according to their ability, yes, and beyond their ability, they were freely willing, imploring us with much urgency that we would receive the gift and the fellowship of the ministering to the saints. And not only as we had hoped, but they first gave themselves to the Lord, and then to us by the will of God. So we urged Titus, that as he had begun, so he would also complete this grace in you as well. (NKJV)

We Must Give As The Early Christians Gave

Acts 4:32–35

Now the multitude of those who believed were of one heart and one soul; neither did anyone say that any of the things he possessed was his own, but they had all things in common. And with great power the apostles gave witness to the resurrection of the Lord Jesus. And great grace was upon them all. Nor was there anyone among them who lacked; for all who were possessors of lands or houses sold them, and brought the proceeds of the things that were sold, and laid them at the apostles' feet; and they distributed to each as anyone had need. (NKJV)

We Must Give As The Jewish People under the Eighth King of Judah, King Joash, Gave

2 Chronicles 24:10–14

Then all the leaders and all the people rejoiced, brought their contributions, and put them into the chest until all had given. So it was, at that time, when the chest was brought to the king's official by the hand of the Levites, and when they saw that there was much money, that the king's scribe and the high priest's officer came and emptied the chest, and took it and returned it to its place. Thus they did day by day, and gathered money in abundance. The king and Jehoiada gave it to those who did the work of the service of the house of the LORD; and they hired masons and carpenters to repair the house of the LORD, and also those who worked in iron and bronze to restore the house of the LORD. So the workmen labored, and the work was completed by them; they restored the house of God to its original condition and reinforced it. When they had finished, they brought the rest of the money before the king and Jehoiada; they made from it articles for the house of the LORD, articles for serving and offering, spoons and vessels of gold and silver. And they offered burnt offerings in the house of the LORD continually all the days of Jehoiada. (NKJV)

WE MUST GIVE AS THE JEWISH PEOPLE UNDER THE THIRTEENTH KING OF JUDAH, KING HEZEKIAH, GAVE

2 Chronicles 31:5–10

As soon as the commandment was circulated, the children of Israel brought in abundance the firstfruits of grain and wine, oil and honey, and of all the produce of the field; and they brought in abundantly the tithe of everything. And the children of Israel and Judah, who dwelt in the cities of Judah, brought the tithe of oxen and sheep; also the tithe of holy things which were consecrated to the LORD their God they laid in heaps. In the third month they began laying them in heaps, and they finished in the seventh month. And when Hezekiah and the leaders came and saw the heaps, they blessed the LORD and His people Israel. Then Hezekiah questioned the priests and the Levites concerning the heaps. And Azariah the chief priest, from the house of Zadok, answered him and said, "Since the people began to bring the offerings into the house of the LORD, we have had enough to eat and have plenty left, for the LORD has blessed His people; and what is left is this great abundance." (NKJV)

WE MUST GIVE AS THE JEWS UNDER THE GOVERNOR OF JERUSALEM, NEHEMIAH, GAVE

Nehemiah 7:70–72

And some of the heads of the fathers' houses gave to the work. The governor gave to the treasury one thousand gold drachmas, fifty basins, and five hundred and thirty priestly garments. Some of the heads of the fathers' houses gave to the treasury of the work twenty thousand gold drachmas, and two thousand two hundred silver minas. And that which the rest of the people gave was twenty thousand gold drachmas, two thousand silver minas, and sixty-seven priestly garments. (NKJV)

WE MUST GIVE AS THE POOR WIDOW WHO GAVE HER ALL

Mark 12:41–44

Now Jesus sat opposite the treasury and saw how the people put money into the treasury. And many who were rich put in much. Then one poor widow came and threw in two mites, which make a quadrans. So He called His disciples to Himself and said to them, "Assuredly, I say to you that this poor widow has put in more than all those who have given to the treasury; for they all put in out of their abundance, but she out of her poverty put in all that she had, her whole livelihood." (NKJV)

Luke 21:1–4

And He looked up and saw the rich putting their gifts into the treasury, and He saw also a certain poor widow putting in two mites. So He said, "Truly I say to you that this poor widow has put in more than all; for all these out of their abundance have put in offerings for God, but she out of her poverty put in all the livelihood that she had." (NKJV)

WE MUST GIVE AS THE PRODIGAL SON'S FATHER IN THE PARABLE OF CHRIST GAVE

Luke 15:22–24

"But the father said to his servants, 'Bring out the best robe and put it on him, and put a ring on his hand and sandals on his feet. And bring the fatted calf here and kill it, and let us eat and be merry; for this my son was dead and is alive again; he was lost and is found.' And they began to be merry." (NKJV)

We Must Give As The Wealthy Tax Collector, Zacchaeus, Gave

Luke 19:1–10

Then Jesus entered and passed through Jericho. Now behold, there was a man named Zacchaeus who was a chief tax collector, and he was rich. And he sought to see who Jesus was, but could not because of the crowd, for he was of short stature. So he ran ahead and climbed up into a sycamore tree to see Him, for He was going to pass that way. And when Jesus came to the place, He looked up and saw him, and said to him, "Zacchaeus, make haste and come down, for today I must stay at your house." So he made haste and came down, and received Him joyfully. But when they saw it, they all complained, saying, "He has gone to be a guest with a man who is a sinner." Then Zacchaeus stood and said to the Lord, "Look, Lord, I give half of my goods to the poor; and if I have taken anything from anyone by false accusation, I restore fourfold." And Jesus said to him, "Today salvation has come to this house, because he also is a son of Abraham; for the Son of Man has come to seek and to save that which was lost." (NKJV)

We Must Give As The Wise Men of the East, the Magi, Gave

Matthew 2:11

And when they had come into the house, they saw the young Child with Mary His mother, and fell down and worshiped Him. And when they had opened their treasures, they presented gifts to Him: gold, frankincense, and myrrh. (NKJV)

We Must Give As The Women of Shunem, Befriender of Elisha, Gave

2 Kings 4:8–10

Now it happened one day that Elisha went to Shunem, where there was a notable woman, and she persuaded him to eat some food. So it was, as often as he passed by, he would turn in there to eat some food. And she said to her husband, "Look now, I know that this is a holy man of God, who passes by us regularly. Please, let us make a small upper room on the wall; and let us put a bed for him there, and a table and a chair and a lampstand; so it will be, whenever he comes to us, he can turn in there." (NKJV)

We Must Give As The Women Friends and Converts of Jesus Gave

Luke 8:1–3

Now it came to pass, afterward, that He went through every city and village, preaching and bringing the glad tidings of the kingdom of God. And the twelve were with Him, and certain women who had been healed of evil spirits and infirmities—Mary called Magdalene, out of whom had come seven demons, and Joanna the wife of Chuza, Herod's steward, and Susanna, and many others who provided for Him from their substance. (NKJV)

We Must Give As The Zarephath Widow Gave

1 Kings 17:7–16

And it happened after a while that the brook dried up, because there had been no rain in the land. Then the word of the LORD came to him, saying, "Arise, go to Zarephath, which belongs to Sidon, and dwell there. See, I have commanded a widow there to provide for you." So he arose and went to Zarephath. And when he came to the gate of the city, indeed a widow was there gathering sticks. And he called to her and said, "Please bring me a little water in a cup, that I may drink." And as she was going to get it, he called to her and said, "Please bring me a morsel of bread in your hand." So she said, "As the LORD your God lives, I do not have bread, only a handful of flour in a bin, and a little oil in a jar; and see, I am gathering a couple of sticks that I may go in and prepare it for myself and my son, that we may eat it, and die." And Elijah said to her, "Do not fear; go and do as you have said, but make me a small cake from it first, and bring it to me; and afterward make some for yourself and your son. For thus says the LORD God of Israel: 'The bin of flour shall not be used up, nor shall the jar of oil run dry, until the day the LORD sends rain on the earth.' " So she went away and did according to the word of Elijah; and she and he and her household ate for many days. The bin of flour was not used up, nor did the jar of oil run dry, according to the word of the LORD which He spoke by Elijah. (NKJV)

WE MUST GIVE AS DAVID, THE KING, BELOVED OF GOD, GAVE

1 Chronicles 29:1–9

Furthermore King David said to all the assembly: "My son Solomon, whom alone God has chosen, is young and inexperienced; and the work is great, because the temple is not for man but for the LORD God. Now for the house of my God I have prepared with all my might: gold for things to be made of gold, silver for things of silver, bronze for things of bronze, iron for things of iron, wood for things of wood, onyx stones, stones to be set, glistening stones of various colors, all kinds of precious stones, and marble slabs in abundance. Moreover, because I have set my affection on the house of my God, I have given to the house of my God, over and above all that I have prepared for the holy house, my own special treasure of gold and silver: three thousand talents of gold, of the gold of Ophir, and seven thousand talents of refined silver, to overlay the walls of the houses; the gold for things of gold and the silver for things of silver, and for all kinds of work to be done by the hands of craftsmen. Who then is willing to consecrate himself this day to the LORD?" Then the leaders of the fathers' houses, leaders of the tribes of Israel, the captains of thousands and of hundreds, with the officers over the king's work, offered willingly. They gave for the work of the house of God five thousand talents and ten thousand darics of gold, ten thousand talents of silver, eighteen thousand talents of bronze, and one hundred thousand talents of iron. And whoever had precious stones gave them to the treasury of the house of the LORD, into the hand of Jehiel the Gershonite. Then the people rejoiced, for they had offered willingly, because with a loyal heart they had offered willingly to the LORD; and King David also rejoiced greatly. (NKJV)

WE MUST GIVE AS EZRA, TEACHER, PRIEST, WRITER, AND DESCENDANT OF AARON GAVE

Ezra 7:15–23

And whereas you are to carry the silver and gold which the king and his counselors have freely offered to the God of Israel, whose dwelling is in Jerusalem; and whereas all the silver and gold that you may find in all the province of Babylon, along with the freewill offering of the people and the priests, are to be freely offered for the house of their God in Jerusalem—now therefore, be careful to buy with this money bulls, rams, and lambs, with their grain offerings and their drink offerings, and offer them on the altar of the house of your God in Jerusalem. And whatever seems good to you and your brethren to do with the rest of the silver and the gold, do it according to the will of your God. Also the articles that are given to you for the service of the house of your God, deliver in full before the God of Jerusalem. And whatever more may be needed for the house of your God, which you may have occasion to provide, pay for it from the king's treasury. And I, even I, Artaxerxes the king, do issue a decree to all the treasurers who are in the region beyond the River, that whatever Ezra the priest, the scribe of the Law of the God of heaven, may require of you, let it be done diligently, up to one hundred talents of silver, one hundred kors of wheat, one hundred baths of wine, one hundred baths of oil, and salt without prescribed limit. Whatever is commanded by the God of heaven, let it diligently be done for the house of the God of heaven. For why should there be wrath against the realm of the king and his sons? (NKJV)

WE MUST GIVE AS HAGGAI, OLD TESTAMENT PROPHET, GAVE

Haggai 1:3–11

Then the word of the LORD came by Haggai the prophet, saying, "Is it time for you yourselves to dwell in your paneled houses, and this temple to lie in ruins?" Now therefore, thus says the LORD of hosts: "Consider your ways! You have sown much, and bring in little; you eat, but do not have enough; you drink, but you are not filled with drink; you clothe yourselves, but no one is warm; and he who earns wages, earns wages to put into a bag with holes." Thus says the LORD of hosts: "Consider your ways! Go up to the mountains and bring wood and build the temple, that I may take pleasure in it and be glorified," says the LORD. You looked for much, but indeed it came to little; and when you brought it home, I blew it away. Why?" says the LORD of hosts. "Because of My house that is in ruins, while every one of you runs to his own house. Therefore the heavens above you withhold the dew, and the earth withholds its fruit. For I called for a drought on the land and the mountains, on the grain and the new wine and the oil, on whatever the ground brings forth, on men and livestock, and on all the labor of your hands." (NKJV)

We Must Give As Hezekiah, King of Judah, Gave

2 Chronicles 31:3–6

The king also appointed a portion of his possessions for the burnt offerings: for the morning and evening burnt offerings, the burnt offerings for the Sabbaths and the New Moons and the set feasts, as it is written in the Law of the LORD. Moreover he commanded the people who dwelt in Jerusalem to contribute support for the priests and the Levites, that they might devote themselves to the Law of the LORD. As soon as the commandment was circulated, the children of Israel brought in abundance the firstfruits of grain and wine, oil and honey, and of all the produce of the field; and they brought in abundantly the tithe of everything. And the children of Israel and Judah, who dwelt in the cities of Judah, brought the tithe of oxen and sheep; also the tithe of holy things which were consecrated to the LORD their God they laid in heaps. (NKJV)

We Must Give As Joash, Eighth King of Judah, Gave

2 Kings 12:1–16

In the seventh year of Jehu, Jehoash became king, and he reigned forty years in Jerusalem. His mother's name was Zibiah of Beersheba. Jehoash did what was right in the sight of the LORD all the days in which Jehoiada the priest instructed him. But the high places were not taken away; the people still sacrificed and burned incense on the high places. And Jehoash said to the priests, "All the money of the dedicated gifts that are brought into the house of the LORD—each man's census money, each man's assessment money—and all the money that a man purposes in his heart to bring into the house of the LORD, let the priests take it themselves, each from his constituency; and let them repair the damages of the temple, wherever any dilapidation is found." Now it was so, by the twenty-third year of

King Jehoash, that the priests had not repaired the damages of the temple. So King Jehoash called Jehoiada the priest and the other priests, and said to them, "Why have you not repaired the damages of the temple? Now therefore, do not take more money from your constituency, but deliver it for repairing the damages of the temple." And the priests agreed that they would neither receive any more money from the people, nor repair the damages of the temple. Then Jehoiada the priest took a chest, bored a hole in its lid, and set it beside the altar, on the right side as one comes into the house of the LORD; and the priests who kept the door put there all the money brought into the house of the LORD. So it was, whenever they saw that there was much money in the chest, that the king's scribe and the high priest came up and put it in bags, and counted the money that was found in the house of the LORD. Then they gave the money, which had been apportioned, into the hands of those who did the work, who had the oversight of the house of the LORD; and they paid it out to the carpenters and builders who worked on the house of the LORD, and to masons and stonecutters, and for buying timber and hewn stone, to repair the damage of the house of the LORD, and for all that was paid out to repair the temple. However there were not made for the house of the LORD basins of silver, trimmers, sprinkling-bowls, trumpets, any articles of gold or articles of silver, from the money brought into the house of the LORD. But they gave that to the workmen, and they repaired the house of the LORD with it. Moreover they did not require an account from the men into whose hand they delivered the money to be paid to workmen, for they dealt faithfully. The money from the trespass offerings and the money from the sin offerings was not brought into the house of the LORD. It belonged to the priests. (NKJV)

We Must Give As King Solomon, the Wise King of Israel, Gave

1 Kings 10:23–25

So King Solomon surpassed all the kings of the earth in riches and wisdom. Now all the earth sought the presence of Solomon to hear his wisdom, which God had put in his heart. Each man brought his present: articles of silver and gold, garments, armor, spices, horses, and mules, at a set rate year by year. (NKJV)

We Must Give As Moses, Hebrew Prophet and Leader, Gave

Exodus 35:4–7

And Moses spoke to all the congregation of the children of Israel, saying, "This is the thing which the LORD commanded, saying: 'Take from among you an offering to the LORD. Whoever is of a willing heart, let him bring it as an offering to the LORD: gold, silver, and bronze; blue , purple, and scarlet thread, fine linen, and goats' hair; ram skins dyed red, badger skins, and acacia wood. (NKJV)

Exodus 36:3–7

And they received from Moses all the offering which the children of Israel had brought for the work of the service of making the sanctuary. So they continued bringing to him freewill offerings every morning. Then all the craftsmen who were doing all the work of the sanctuary came, each from the work he was doing, and they spoke to Moses, saying, "The people bring much more than enough for the service of the work which the LORD commanded us to do." So Moses gave a commandment, and they caused it to be proclaimed throughout the camp, saying, "Let neither man nor woman do any more work for the offering of the sanctuary." And the people were restrained from bring-

ing, for the material they had was sufficient for all the work to be done—indeed too much. (NKJV)

WE MUST GIVE AS NEHEMIAH, GOVERNOR OF JERUSALEM, GAVE

Nehemiah 10:32–39

Also we made ordinances for ourselves, to exact from ourselves yearly one-third of a shekel for the service of the house of our God: for the showbread, for the regular grain offering, for the regular burnt offering of the Sabbaths, the New Moons, and the set feasts; for the holy things, for the sin offerings to make atonement for Israel, and all the work of the house of our God. We cast lots among the priests, the Levites, and the people, for bringing the wood offering into the house of our God, according to our fathers' houses, at the appointed times year by year, to burn on the altar of the LORD our God as it is written in the Law. And we made ordinances to bring the firstfruits of our ground and the firstfruits of all fruit of all trees, year by year, to the house of the LORD; to bring the firstborn of our sons and our cattle, as it is written in the Law, and the firstborn of our herds and our flocks, to the house of our God, to the priests who minister in the house of our God; to bring the firstfruits of our dough, our offerings, the fruit from all kinds of trees, the new wine and oil, to the priests, to the storerooms of the house of our God; and to bring the tithes of our land to the Levites, for the Levites should receive the tithes in all our farming communities. And the priest, the descendant of Aaron, shall be with the Levites when the Levites receive tithes; and the Levites shall bring up a tenth of the tithes to the house of our God, to the rooms of the storehouse. For the children of Israel and the children of Levi shall bring the offering of the grain, of the new wine and the oil, to the storerooms where the articles of the sanctuary are, where the priests who minister and the gatekeepers and the singers are; and we will not neglect the house of our God. (NKJV)

Nehemiah 12:44–47

And at the same time some were appointed over the rooms of the storehouse for the offerings, the firstfruits, and the tithes, to gather into them from the fields of the cities the portions specified by the Law for the priests and Levites; for Judah rejoiced over the priests and Levites who ministered. Both the singers and the gatekeepers kept the charge of their God and the charge of the purification, according to the command of David and Solomon his son. For in the days of David and Asaph of old there were chiefs of the singers, and songs of praise and thanksgiving to God. In the days of Zerubbabel and in the days of Nehemiah all Israel gave the portions for the singers and the gatekeepers, a portion for each day. They also consecrated holy things for the Levites, and the Levites consecrated them for the children of Aaron. (NKJV)

WE MUST GIVE AS PAUL, INFLUENTIAL JEWISH APOSTLE, GAVE

1 Corinthians 16:1–4

Now concerning the collection for the saints, as I have given orders to the churches of Galatia, so you must do also: On the first day of the week let each one of you lay something aside, storing up as he may prosper, that there be no collections when I come. And when I come, whomever you approve by your letters I will send to bear your gift to Jerusalem. But if it is fitting that I go also, they will go with me. (NKJV)

2 Corinthians 8:9

For you know the grace of our Lord Jesus Christ, that though He was rich, yet for your sakes He became poor, that you through His poverty might become rich. (NKJV)

Philippians 4:14–19

Nevertheless you have done well that you shared in my distress. Now you Philippians know also that in the beginning of the gospel, when I departed from Macedonia, no church shared with me concerning giving and receiving but you only. For even in Thessalonica you sent aid once and again for my necessities. Not that I seek the gift, but I seek the fruit that abounds to your account. Indeed I have all and abound. I am full, having received from Epaphroditus the things sent from you, a sweet-smelling aroma, an acceptable sacrifice, well pleasing to God. And my God shall supply all your need according to His riches in glory by Christ Jesus. (NKJV)

WE MUST GIVE AS THE APOSTLES OF THE NEW TESTAMENT GAVE

Acts 4:34–37

Nor was there anyone among them who lacked; for all who were possessors of lands or houses sold them, and brought the proceeds of the things that were sold, and laid them at the apostles' feet; and they distributed to each as anyone had need. And Joses, who was also named Barnabas by the apostles (which is translated Son of Encouragement), a Levite of the country of Cyprus, having land, sold it, and brought the money and laid it at the apostles' feet. (NKJV)

WE MUST GIVE AS THE BUSINESSPERSON WHO GAVE HIS SERVANTS TALENTS GAVE

Matthew 25:14–30

"For the kingdom of heaven is like a man traveling to a far country, who called his own servants and delivered his goods to them. And to one he gave five talents, to another two, and to another one, to each according to his own ability; and im-

mediately he went on a journey. Then he who had received the five talents went and traded with them, and made another five talents. And likewise he who had received two gained two more also. But he who had received one went and dug in the ground, and hid his lord's money. After a long time the lord of those servants came and settled accounts with them. So he who had received five talents came and brought five other talents, saying, 'Lord, you delivered to me five talents; look, I have gained five more talents besides them.' "His lord said to him, 'Well done, good and faithful servant; you were faithful over a few things, I will make you ruler over many things. Enter into the joy of your lord.' "He also who had received two talents came and said, 'Lord, you delivered to me two talents; look, I have gained two more talents besides them.' "His lord said to him, 'Well done, good and faithful servant; you have been faithful over a few things, I will make you ruler over many things. Enter into the joy of your lord.' "Then he who had received the one talent came and said, 'Lord, I knew you to be a hard man, reaping where you have not sown, and gathering where you have not scattered seed. And I was afraid, and went and hid your talent in the ground. Look, there you have what is yours.' "But his lord answered and said to him, 'You wicked and lazy servant, you knew that I reap where I have not sown, and gather where I have not scattered seed. So you ought to have deposited my money with the bankers, and at my coming I would have received back my own with interest. Therefore take the talent from him, and give it to him who has ten talents. For to everyone who has, more will be given, and he will have abundance; but from him who does not have, even what he has will be taken away. And cast the unprofitable servant into the outer darkness. There will be weeping and gnashing of teeth.'" (NKJV)

CHAPTER 8

How God Blesses Our Stewardship

8 EXAMPLES OF STEWARDSHIP GIVING

1. God provides with plenty left over.

2 Chronicles 31:9–10

And Azariah the chief priest, from the house of Zadok, answered him and said, "Since the people began to bring the offerings into the house of the LORD, we have had enough to eat and have plenty left, for the LORD has blessed His people; and what is left is this great abundance." (NKJV)

2. If I am a faithful steward, God allows me to manage His resources.

Psalm 24:1

The earth is the LORD's, and all its fullness, the world and those who dwell therein. (NKJV)

Proverbs 3:9–10

Honor the LORD with your possessions, and with the firstfruits of all your increase; so your barns will be filled with plenty, and your vats will overflow with new wine. (NKJV)

Proverbs 11:24–25, 28

There is one who scatters, yet increases more; and there is one who withholds more than is right, but it leads to poverty. The generous soul will be made rich, and he who waters will also be watered himself. He who trusts in his riches will fall, but the righteous will flourish like foliage. (NKJV)

Proverbs 22:9

He who has a generous eye will be blessed, for he gives of his bread to the poor. (NKJV)

Proverbs 28:27

He who gives to the poor will not lack, but he who hides his eyes will have many curses. (NKJV)

Leviticus 25:23

The land shall not be sold permanently, for the land is Mine; for you are strangers and sojourners with Me. (NKJV)

Haggai 2:8

"The silver is Mine, and the gold is Mine," says the LORD of hosts. (NKJV)

1 Corinthians 6:19–20

Or do you not know that your body is the temple of the Holy Spirit who is in you, whom you have from God, and you are not your own? For you were bought at a price; therefore glorify God in your body and in your spirit, which are God's. (NKJV)

John 3:16

"For God so loved the world that He gave His only begotten Son, that whoever believes in Him should not perish but have everlasting life." (NKJV)

Deuteronomy 8:18

And you shall remember the LORD your God, for it is He who gives you power to get wealth, that He may establish His covenant which He swore to your fathers, as it is this day. (NKJV)

1 Corinthians 4:2

Moreover it is required in stewards that one be found faithful. (NKJV)

Romans 14:10–12

But why do you judge your brother? Or why do you show contempt for your brother? For we shall all stand before the judgment seat of Christ. For it is written: "As I live, says the LORD, every knee shall bow to Me, And every tongue shall confess to God." So then each of us shall give account of himself to God. (NKJV)

3. Where I place my money indicates where my heart is.

Ecclesiastes 5:12

The sleep of a laboring man is sweet, Whether he eats little or much; but the abundance of the rich will not permit him to sleep. (NKJV)

Matthew 6:19–21

Do not lay up for yourselves treasures on earth, where moth and rust destroy and where thieves break in and steal; but lay up for yourselves treasures in heaven, where neither moth nor rust destroys and where thieves do not break in and steal. For where your treasure is, there your heart will be also. (NKJV)

4. Earth is not my final resting place.

Philippians 3:20

For our citizenship is in heaven, from which we also eagerly wait for the Savior, the Lord Jesus Christ. (NKJV)

Psalm 90:10

The days of our lives are seventy years; And if by reason of strength they are eighty years, yet their boast is only labor and sorrow; for it is soon cut off, and we fly away. (NKJV)

Psalm 39:5b

Certainly every man at his best state is but vapor. (NKJV)

5. I live in a temporary moment. Eternity is forever.

Hebrews 11:25–26

Choosing rather to suffer affliction with the people of God than to enjoy the passing pleasures of sin, esteeming the reproach of Christ greater riches than the treasures in Egypt; for he looked to the reward. (NKJV)

Matthew 25:21

"His lord said to him, 'Well done, good and faithful servant; you were faithful over a few things, I will make you ruler over many things. Enter into the joy of your lord.'" (NKJV)

6. Generosity is the antidote to personal greed.

Ecclesiastes 5:10, 13–14

He who loves silver will not be satisfied with silver; Nor he who loves abundance, with increase. This also is vanity. There is a severe evil which I have seen under the sun: Riches kept for their owner to his hurt. But those riches perish through misfortune; When he begets a son, there is nothing in his hand. (NKJV)

1 Timothy 6:9–10

But those who desire to be rich fall into temptation and a snare, and into many foolish and harmful lusts which drown men in destruction and perdition. For the love of money is a root of all kinds of evil, for which some have strayed from the faith in their greediness, and pierced themselves through with many sorrows. (NKJV)

1 Timothy 6:17–18

Command those who are rich in this present age not to be haughty, nor to trust in uncertain riches but in the living God, who gives us richly all things to enjoy. Let them do good, that they be rich in good works, ready to give, willing to share. (NKJV)

7. I am blessed to become a blessing to others.

Malachi 3:10b

"And try Me now in this," Says the LORD of hosts, "If I will not open for you the windows of heaven and pour out for you such blessing that there will not be room enough to receive it." (NKJV)

Luke 6:38

"Give, and it will be given to you: good measure, pressed down, shaken together, and running over will be put into your bosom. For with the same measure that you use, it will be measured back to you." (NKJV)

Luke 12:33

"Sell what you have and give alms; provide yourselves money bags which do not grow old, a treasure in the heavens that does not fail, where no thief approaches nor moth destroys." (NKJV)

Acts 20:35

"I have shown you in every way, by laboring like this, that you must support the weak. And remember the words of the Lord Jesus, that He said, 'It is more blessed to give than to receive.'" (NKJV)

2 Corinthians 8:7

But as you abound in everything — in faith, in speech, in knowledge, in all diligence, and in your love for us — see that you abound in this grace also. (NKJV)

2 Corinthians 9:7

So let each one give as he purposes in his heart, not grudgingly or of necessity; for God loves a cheerful giver. (NKJV)

2 Corinthians 9:10–13

Now may He who supplies seed to the sower, and bread for food, supply and multiply the seed you have sown and increase the fruits of your righteousness, while you are enriched in everything for all liberality, which causes thanksgiving through us

*to God. For the administration of this service not only supplies
the needs of the saints, but also is abounding through many
thanksgivings to God, while, through the proof of this ministry, they glorify God for the obedience of your confession to the
gospel of Christ, and for your liberal sharing with them and all
men, (NKJV)*

8. Money CAN buy happiness.

Let me give you a possible scenario for buying personal happiness. What if your total income were fifty thousand dollars a year?
And let's agree that you are by now a faithful and obedient tithe
payer (i.e. you give God 10 percent of your increase and you have
become a good steward of the 90 percent He has entrusted you
with). Obviously, if you are a good manager, you are already living comfortably below the 90 percent remainder. Now let's suppose
that you work for someone else and you receive a five-thousand-
dollar raise in your annual income. What should you do with that?
Should you buy a newer car? How about take a longer vacation?
Maybe you could buy more "stuff" so that you need a bigger garage or a larger shed to store it in.

Consider the "happiness" alternative. Instead of using the money to heap new "stuff" upon yourself, why not use the additional
increase to help others? Here are a few ideas for you:

$ 5,000	Increase in Personal Income
$ 500	additional tithe to your local church
$ 1,200	support a missionary $100 per month
$ 500	support a homeless shelter
$ 300	pay some utility bills of an unemployed person
$ 500	donate to a food program for the needy
$ 500	arrange for a poor family to enjoy a nice Christmas
$ 1,000	help a college student with tuition and/or books
$ 400	buy new tires for an older person on a fixed income
$ 100	give to a neighborhood child to help with summer camp
$ 0	Balance of Increase

Try this one time with your increase, and just see whether or not you receive more joy and happiness then you've ever experienced before. Honor the Lord with your increase; honor the Lord with your wealth. The principle of enlarged measure begins with the gift of giving.

Isaiah 58:10–11

If you extend your soul to the hungry and satisfy the afflicted soul, then your light shall dawn in the darkness, and your darkness shall be as the noonday. The LORD will guide you continually, and satisfy your soul in drought, and strengthen your bones; you shall be like a watered garden, and like a spring of water, whose waters do not fail. (NKJV)

Malachi 3:10

Bring all the tithes into the storehouse, that there may be food in My house, And try Me now in this," says the LORD of hosts, "If I will not open for you the windows of heaven and pour out for you such blessing that there will not be room enough to receive it. (NKJV)

Matthew 10:42

"And whoever gives one of these little ones only a cup of cold water in the name of a disciple, assuredly, I say to you, he shall by no means lose his reward." (NKJV)

Matthew 25:21

"His lord said to him, 'Well done, good and faithful servant; you were faithful over a few things, I will make you ruler over many things. Enter into the joy of your lord.'" (NKJV)

Matthew 25:34–36

"Then the King will say to those on His right hand, 'Come, you blessed of My Father, inherit the kingdom prepared for you from the foundation of the world: for I was hungry and you gave Me food; I was thirsty and you gave Me drink; I was a stranger and you took Me in; I was naked and you clothed Me; I was sick and you visited Me; I was in prison and you came to Me.'" (NKJV)

Luke 6:38

"Give, and it will be given to you: good measure, pressed down, shaken together, and running over will be put into your bosom. For with the same measure that you use, it will be measured back to you." (NKJV)

Luke 16:9–11

"And I say to you, make friends for yourselves by unrighteous mammon, that when you fail, they may receive you into an everlasting home. He who is faithful in what is least is faithful also in much; and he who is unjust in what is least is unjust also in much. Therefore if you have not been faithful in the unrighteous mammon, who will commit to your trust the true riches?" (NKJV)

Luke 18:28–30

Then Peter said, "See, we have left all and followed You." So He said to them, "Assuredly, I say to you, there is no one who has left house or parents or brothers or wife or children, for the sake of the kingdom of God, who shall not receive many times more in this present time, and in the age to come eternal life." (NKJV)

Acts 20:35

I have shown you in every way, by laboring like this, that you must support the weak. And remember the words of the Lord Jesus, that He said, "It is more blessed to give than to receive." (NKJV)

2 Corinthians 9:7–11

So let each one give as he purposes in his heart, not grudgingly or of necessity; for God loves a cheerful giver. And God is able to make all grace abound toward you, that you, always having all sufficiency in all things, may have an abundance for every good work. As it is written: "He has dispersed abroad, He has given to the poor; His righteousness endures forever." Now may He who supplies seed to the sower, and bread for food, supply and multiply the seed you have sown and increase the fruits of your righteousness, while you are enriched in everything for all liberality, which causes thanksgiving through us to God. (NKJV)

Philippians 4:14–19

Nevertheless you have done well that you shared in my distress. Now you Philippians know also that in the beginning of the gospel, when I departed from Macedonia, no church shared with me concerning giving and receiving but you only. For even in Thessalonica you sent aid once and again for my necessities. Not that I seek the gift, but I seek the fruit that abounds to your account. Indeed I have all and abound. I am full, having received from Epaphroditus the things sent from you, a sweet-smelling aroma, an acceptable sacrifice, well pleasing to God. And my God shall supply all your need according to His riches in glory by Christ Jesus. (NKJV)

Hebrews 11:25–26

Choosing rather to suffer affliction with the people of God than to enjoy the passing pleasures of sin, esteeming the reproach of Christ greater riches than the treasures in Egypt; for he looked to the reward. (NKJV)

1 Timothy 6:17–19

Command those who are rich in this present age not to be haughty, nor to trust in uncertain riches but in the living God, who gives us richly all things to enjoy. Let them do good, that they be rich in good works, ready to give, willing to share, storing up for themselves a good foundation for the time to come, that they may lay hold on eternal life. (NKJV)

Source Material

21 Unbreakable Laws of Success, Max Anders, Thomas Nelson, 1996

A Christian Guide to Prosperity; Fries & Taylor, California: Communications Research, 1984

A Look At Stewardship, Word Aflame Publications, 2001

American Savings Education Council (http://www.asec.org)

Anointed For Business, Ed Silvoso, Regal, 2002

Avoiding Common Financial Mistakes, Ron Blue, Navpress, 1991

Baker Encyclopedia of the Bible; Walter Elwell, Michigan: Baker Book House, 1988

Becoming The Best, Barry Popplewell, England: Gower Publishing Company Limited, 1988

Business Proverbs, Steve Marr, Fleming H. Revell, 2001

Cheapskate Monthly, Mary Hunt

Commentary on the Old Testament; Keil-Delitzsch, Michigan: Eerdmans Publishing, 1986

Crown Financial Ministries, various publications

Customers As Partners, Chip Bell, Texas: Berrett-Koehler Publishers, 1994

Cut Your Bills in Half; Pennsylvania: Rodale Press, Inc., 1989

Debt-Free Living, Larry Burkett, Dimensions, 2001

Die Broke, Stephen M. Pollan & Mark Levine, HarperBusiness, 1997

Double Your Profits, Bob Fifer, Virginia: Lincoln Hall Press, 1993

Eerdmans' Handbook to the Bible, Michigan: William B. Eerdmans Publishing Company, 1987

Eight Steps to Seven Figures, Charles B. Carlson, Double Day, 2000

Everyday Life in Bible Times; Washington DC: National Geographic Society, 1967

Financial Dominion, Norvel Hayes, Harrison House, 1986

Financial Freedom, Larry Burkett, Moody Press, 1991

Financial Freedom, Patrick Clements, VMI Publishers, 2003

Financial Peace, Dave Ramsey, Viking Press, 2003

Financial Self-Defense; Charles Givens, New York: Simon And Schuster, 1990

Flood Stage, Oral Roberts, 1981

Generous Living, Ron Blue, Zondervan, 1997

Get It All Done, Tony and Robbie Fanning, New York:Pennsylvania: Chilton Book, 1979

Getting Out of Debt, Howard Dayton, Tyndale House, 1986

Getting Out of Debt, Mary Stephenson, Fact Sheet 436, University of Maryland Cooperative Extension Service, 1988

Giving and Tithing, Larry Burkett, Moody Press, 1991

God's Plan For Giving, John MacArthur, Jr., Moody Press, 1985

God's Will is Prosperity, Gloria Copeland, Harrison House, 1978

Great People of the Bible and How They Lived; New York: Reader's Digest, 1974

How Others Can Help You Get Out of Debt; Esther M. Maddux, Circular 759-3,

How To Make A Business Plan That Works, Henderson, North Island Sound Limited, 1989

How To Manage Your Money, Larry Burkett, Moody Press, 1999

How to Personally Profit From the Laws of Success, Sterling Sill, NIFP, Inc., 1978

How to Plan for Your Retirement; New York: Corrigan & Kaufman, Longmeadow Press, 1985

Is God Your Source?, Oral Roberts, 1992

It's Not Luck, Eliyahu Goldratt, Great Barrington, MA: The North River Press, 1994

Jesus CEO, Laurie Beth Jones, Hyperion, 1995

John Avanzini Answers Your Questions About Biblical Economics, Harrison House, 1992

Living on Less and Liking It More, Maxine Hancock, Chicago, Illinois: Moody Press, 1976

Making It Happen; Charles Conn, New Jersey: Fleming H. Revell Company, 1981

Master Your Money Or It Will Master You, Arlo E. Moehlenpah, Doing Good Ministries, 1999

Master Your Money; Ron Blue, Tennessee: Thomas Nelson, Inc. 1986

Miracle of Seed Faith, Oral Roberts, 1970

Mississippi State University Extension Service

Money, Possessions, and Eternity, Randy Alcorn, Tyndale House, 2003

More Than Enough, David Ramsey, Penguin Putnam Inc, 2002

Moving the Hand of God, John Avanzini, Harrison House, 1990

Multiplication, Tommy Barnett, Creation House, 1997

NebFacts, Nebraska Cooperative Extension

New York Post

One Up On Wall Street; New York: Peter Lynch, Simon And Schuster, 1989

Personal Finances, Larry Burkett, Moody Press, 1991

Portable MBA in Finance and Accounting; Livingstone, Canada: John Wiley & Sons, Inc., 1992

Principle-Centered Leadership, Stephen R. Covey, New York: Summit Books, 1991

Principles of Financial Management, Kolb & DeMong, Texas: Business Publications, Inc., 1988

Rapid Debt Reduction Strategies, John Avanzini, HIS Publishing, 1990

Real Wealth, Wade Cook, Arizona: Regency Books, 1985

See You At The Top, Zig Ziglar, Louisianna: Pelican Publishing Company, 1977

Seed-Faith Commentary on the Holy Bible, Oral Roberts, Pinoak Publications, 1975

Sharkproof, Harvey Mackay, New York: HarperCollins Publishers, 1993

Smart Money, Ken and Daria Dolan, New York: Random House, Inc., 1988

Strong's Concordance, Tennessee: Crusade Bible Publishers, Inc.,

Success by Design, Peter Hirsch, Bethany House, 2002

Success is the Quality of your Journey, Jennifer James, New York: Newmarket Press, 1983

Swim with the Sharks Without Being Eaten Alive, Harvey Mackay, William Morrow , 1988

The Almighty and the Dollar; Jim McKeever, Oregon: Omega Publications, 1981

The Challenge, Robert Allen, New York: Simon And Schuster, 1987

The Family Financial Workbook, Larry Burkett, Moody Press, 2002

The Management Methods of Jesus, Bob Briner, Thomas Nelson, 1996

The Millionaire Next Door, Thomas Stanley & William Danko, Pocket Books, 1996

The Money Book for Kids, Nancy Burgeson, Troll Associates,1992

The Money Book for King's Kids; Harold E. Hill, New Jersey: Fleming H. Revell Company, 1984

The Seven Habits of Highly Effective People, Stephen Covey, New York: Simon And Schuster, 1989

The Wealthy Barber, David Chilton, California: Prima Publishing, 1991

Theological Wordbook of the Old Testament, Chicago, Illinois: Moody Press, 1981

Treasury of Courage and Confidence, Norman Vincent Peale, New York: Doubleday & Co., 1970

True Prosperity, Dick Iverson, Bible Temple Publishing, 1993

Trust God For Your Finances, Jack Hartman, Lamplight Publications, 1983

University of Georgia Cooperative Extension Service, 1985

Virginia Cooperative Extension

Webster's Unabridged Dictionary, Dorset & Baber, 1983

What Is an Entrepreneur; David Robinson, MA: Kogan Page Limited, 1990

Word Meanings in the New Testament, Ralph Earle, Michigan: Baker Book House, 1986

Word Pictures in the New Testament; Robertson, Michigan: Baker Book House, 1930

Word Studies in the New Testament; Vincent, New York: Charles Scribner's Sons, 1914

Worth

You Can Be Financially Free, George Fooshee, Jr., 1976, Fleming H. Revell Company.

Your Key to God's Bank, Rex Humbard, 1977

Your Money Counts, Howard, Dayton, Tyndale House, 1997

Your Money Management, MaryAnn Paynter, Circular 1271, University of Illinois Cooperative Extension Service, 1987.

Your Money Matters, Malcolm MacGregor, Bethany Fellowship, Inc., 1977

Your Road to Recovery, Oral Roberts, Oliver Nelson, 1986

Comments On Sources

Over the years I have collected bits and pieces of interesting material, written notes on sermons I've heard, jotted down comments on financial articles I've read, and gathered a lot of great information. It is unfortunate that I didn't record the sources of all of these notes in my earlier years. I gratefully extend my appreciation to the many writers, authors, teachers and pastors from whose articles and sermons I have gleaned much insight.

Rich Brott

Online Resources

American Savings Education Council (http://www.asec.org)

Bloomberg.com (http://www.bloomberg.com)

Bureau of the Public Debt Online (http://www.publicdebt.treas.gov)

BusinessWeek (http://www.businessweek.com)

Charles Schwab & Co., Inc. (http://www.schwab.com)

Consumer Federation of America (http://www.consumerfed.org)

Debt Advice.org (http://www.debtadvice.org)

Federal Reserve System (http://www.federalreserve.gov)

Fidelity Investments (http://www.fidelity.com)

Financial Planning Association (http://www.fpanet.org)

Forbes (www.forbes.com)

Fortune Magazine (http://www.fortune.com)

Generous Giving (http://www.generousgiving.org/)

Investing for Your Future (http://www.investing.rutgers.edu)

Kiplinger Magazine (http://www.kiplinger.com/)

Money Magazine (http://money.cnn.com)

MorningStar (http://www.morningstar.com)

MSN Money (http://moneycentral.msn.com)

Muriel Siebert (http://www.siebertnet.com)

National Center on Education and the Economy (http://www.ncee.org)

National Foundation for Credit Counseling (http://www.nfcc.org)

Quicken (http://www.quicken.com)

Smart Money (http://www.smartmoney.com)

Social Security Online (http://www.ssa.gov)

Standard & Poor's (http://www2.standardandpoors.com)

The Dollar Stretcher, Gary Foreman, (http://www.stretcher.com)

The Vanguard Group (http://flagship.vanguard.com)

U.S. Securities and Exchange Commission (http://www.sec.gov)

Yahoo! Finance (http://finance.yahoo.com)

Magazine Resources

Business Week
Consumer Reports
Forbes
Kiplinger's Personal Finance
Money
Smart Money
US News and World Report

Newspaper Resources

Barrons
Investors Business Daily
USA Today
Wall Street Journal
Washington Times

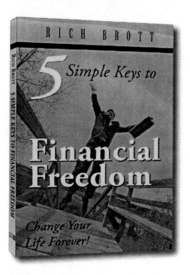

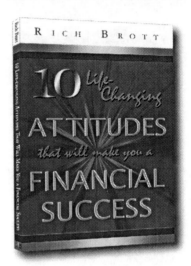

Additional Resources by Rich Brott

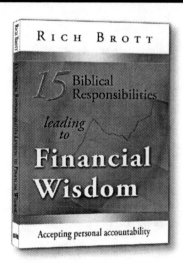

15 Biblical Responsibilities
Leading to Financial Wisdom

Accepting Personal Accountability

By Rich Brott

6" x 9", 120 pages
ISBN 1-60185-010-7
ISBN (EAN) 978-1-60185-010-2

Book Publishing

Order online at:

www.amazon.com
www.barnesandnoble.com
www.booksamillion.com
www.citychristianpublishing.com
www.walmart.com

www.AbcBookPublishing.com

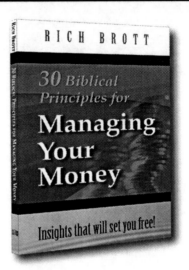

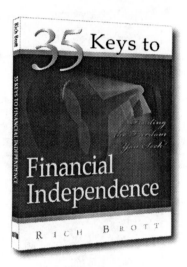

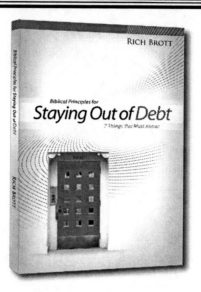

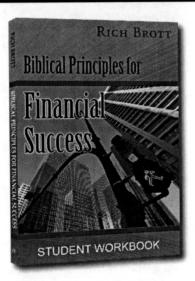

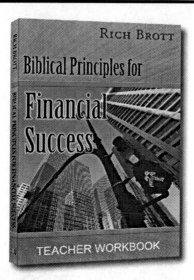

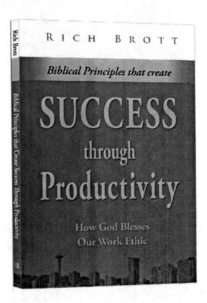

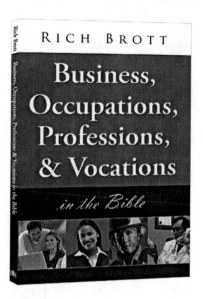

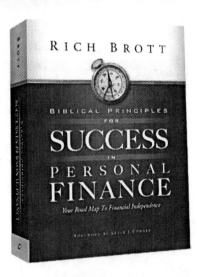

Additional Resources by Rich Brott

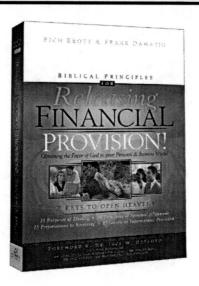

Biblical Principles for Releasing Financial Provision!

*Obtaining the Favor of God in Your
Personal and Business World*

By Rich Brott

7.5" x 10", 456 pages
ISBN 1-59383-021-1
ISBN (EAN) 978-1-59383-021-2

Book Publishing

Order online at:

www.amazon.com
www.barnesandnoble.com
www.booksamillion.com
www.citychristianpublishing.com
www.walmart.com

www.AbcBookPublishing.com

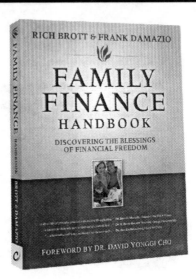

CPSIA information can be obtained at www.ICGtesting.com
Printed in the USA
BVOW02s1955190315

392425BV00003B/5/P